LEARNINGEXPRESS

THE BASICS MADE EASY . . .
IN 20 MINUTES A DAY!

A New Approach to "Mastering The Basics." An innovative 20-step self-study program helps you learn at your own pace and make visible progress in just 20 minutes a day.

GRAMMAR ESSENTIALS
HOW TO STUDY
IMPROVE YOUR WRITING FOR WORK
MATH ESSENTIALS
PRACTICAL SPELLING
PRACTICAL VOCABULARY
READ BETTER, REMEMBER MORE
THE SECRETS OF TAKING ANY TEST

Become a Better Student—*Quickly*
Become a More Marketable Employee—*Fast*
Get a Better Job—*Now*

IMPROVE YOUR WRITING FOR WORK

Second Edition

Elizabeth Chesla

LEARNINGEXPRESS

NEW YORK

Library of Congress Cataloging-in-Publication Data

Chesla, Elizabeth L.
Improve your writing for work / Elizabeth Chesla.—2nd ed.
    p.   cm.
    Rev. ed. of: Improve your writing for work in 20 minutes a day. 1997.
    ISBN 1-57685-337-3 (pbk.)
    1. Business Writing.   I. Chesla, Elizabeth L. Improve your writing for work
in 20 minutes a day.   II. Title.

HF5718.3 .C465 2000
808'.06665—dc21
                             00-058790

Printed in the United States of America
9 8 7 6 5 4 3 2
Second Edition

Permission to reprint granted by:
Creative Change, Inc. All rights reserved. See pages 253-258.
Executive Car Service, Inc. All rights reserved. See pages 263–267.
Gary Bilezikian Design. All rights reserved. See pages 259-262.
Polytechnic University. All rights reserved. See pages 244-252.

For Further Information
For information on LearningExpress, other LearningExpress products, or bulk sales,
please write to us at:
      LearningExpress®
      900 Broadway
      Suite 604
      New York, NY 10003

or visit us at:
      www.learnatest.com

CONTENTS

1   Why You Need This Book 1

Section 1: The Basics of Writing for Work **7**

2   What Is Workplace Writing? 9

3   Clearly Stating Your Main Idea 17

4   Clearly Supporting Your Main Idea 25

5   Organizing Your Ideas 33

6   Readability Strategies 49

Section 2: Getting Your Message Across Clearly **65**

7   Reporting 67

8   Conveying a Positive or Neutral Message 75

9   Conveying a Negative or Unpleasant Message 85

10   Writing Procedures and Instructions 97

11   Reviewing 107

12   Convincing 113

Section 3: Workplace Writing Formats **121**

13   Letters 123

14   Memos 137

15   Reports 149

16   Proposals 159

17   Electronic Mail 167

18   Websites 179

Section 4: Tips for an Easy Read **193**

19   Introductions and Conclusions 195

20   Writing Clearly 203

21   Writing with Style 213

22   Revising Strategies 223

23   Editing Strategies 233

Appendix A: *Writing Samples from the Workplace* 243

Appendix B: *Additional Resources* 269

Index 275

IMPROVE YOUR WRITING FOR WORK

Second Edition

CHAPTER | 1

Some people break into a cold sweat at the thought of having to write anything official or formal, like a memo or report for work. Others might not be so intimidated, but they still need help in getting their ideas down on paper. Are you one of those people? Then this book is for you.

WHY YOU NEED THIS BOOK

"Most business and government executives, when cornered, will tell you that writing is probably the most important single skill … [a] person can have."

Jefferson Bates

Who would have thought you'd have to do so much writing at work? Reports, evaluations, equipment requisitions, e-mails, letters and memos—even if you're not a manager (yet), you end up writing more—and more often—than you would have ever imagined. Not only that, but you're often judged by how well you express yourself in writing.

Whatever your job title or position, you need to be able to get your ideas across clearly and correctly, in the form that's expected in your workplace. Effective writing will help you succeed in your present job and help prepare you for the next step ahead.

This book is for you if you:

- Have to write for your job, even if only occasionally
- Get nervous when you have to write something
- Don't always know how to put your ideas down on paper
- Sometimes have trouble figuring out just what ideas *belong* on that piece of paper
- Have trouble getting started or deciding how to end
- Can't always figure out how to organize your ideas
- Worry about what other people think of your writing
- Need to improve your writing skills for work or school

HOW TO USE THIS BOOK

The chapters in this book are designed to help you better meet the challenges of writing for work. Each chapter focuses on a single aspect of writing in the workplace, so that you can complete a chapter in approximately 20 minutes. If you complete one chapter a day, Monday through Friday, and do all the exercises carefully, you should become a much more powerful and effective writer (and thinker) by the end of your period of study.

Although each chapter can serve as an effective skill builder on its own, it is important that you proceed through this book in order, from Chapter 1 to Chapter 23. For example, the first two sections (Chapters 2–12) cover the basics of workplace writing: the fundamental principles and strategies that make the difference between good and bad communication. Each chapter builds upon skills and ideas discussed in previous chapters, so if you don't have a thorough understanding of the concepts taught in Section 1, you won't get the full benefit of Section 2. This is true of each chapter as well as each section, so please be sure you thoroughly understand each chapter before moving on to the next one.

The book is divided into four sections of closely related chapters. The sections are organized as follows:

- Section 1: The Basics of Writing for Work
- Section 2: Getting Your Message Across Clearly
- Section 3: Workplace Writing Formats
- Section 4: Tips for an Easy Read

Each chapter provides several exercises that allow you to put the skills you learn into immediate practice. Instead of merely checking off the answers in multiple-choice exercises, you'll spend a lot of time *doing your own writing.* Like cooking, writing is a skill that only improves *with practice.* You can read as many cookbooks as you like, but you won't get any better unless you get in the kitchen and practice. The same is true for writing. The more you put your pen to paper (or fingers to keyboard), the more effectively you'll be able to communicate.

As you work through this book, then, make sure you try all of the practice exercises. Keep the answers you write out on separate sheets of paper in a safe place, so you can refer to them in later chapters of the book. To ensure you're on the right track, each chapter provides sample answers and explanations wherever possible. The answers are always *suggested* or *possible* answers. When it comes to real writing, each person's answer will be a little different.

You'll also find practical "Skill Building" ideas in each chapter: simple thinking or writing tasks you can do throughout the day or the week to sharpen the skills you learn in that chapter.

The Best Advice: Get Feedback

Without a doubt, one of the best things you can do to improve your writing skills is to *get feedback.* A common mistake of inexperienced writers is to not pay enough attention to their readers. However, in the world of work, a lack of attention to your audience can not only get you in trouble—it can also put you right out of business.

That's why it's especially important to keep the reader foremost in your mind at all times. After all, writing is communication—and if the person receiving your communication doesn't understand your message, you've failed in your task. By getting feedback, you can help ensure that your message is coming across clearly. Here are two good ways to get feedback.

Read Your Work Out Loud

Before you send out something that you've written, go someplace private where you can read what you've written out loud. Don't just mumble under your breath—read boldly, loudly, and clearly, as if you're reading to an audience. As you read, *listen* to how your words sound. *Hear* what you've written.

When we read silently, we often automatically insert words that aren't actually there on paper, and we tend to skim over sections that seem clear but aren't. However, when you read out loud, you can hear where your wording sounds awkward, or where your sentences are too long or confusing. You can also hear where your writing simply doesn't convey what it needs to or say what you intended.

Reading out loud also helps you get used to your writing "voice"—how you sound on paper. If you read something out loud and it doesn't "sound like you," then you should revise it. Even work-related writing should have personality—yours. And if it sounds false to you, it will probably sound false to your reader, too.

Share Your Work with Someone Else

There's only one sure way to know that something you've written is effective and communicates exactly what you want to convey: *Share it with someone else.* Give a draft copy of your communication to a coworker or someone else you trust. Make sure your reader knows your intended audience, and ask your reader the following questions:

- Is the purpose of what I've written clear?
- Is there anything unclear in what I've written?
- Is there anything you need to know more about?
- Is there anything inappropriate in what I've written?

Listen carefully to your reader's feedback. It's often difficult to accept criticism about your writing, especially at first, but you should listen carefully to what your reader has to say. Critics aren't always right, but chances are if a reader doesn't understand what you've written, or sees a purpose that's different from what you intended, then what you've written needs to be revised.

The Truth About Revising

One of the main reasons people find themselves frustrated with writing is because they feel they should be able to get it right on the first try. "If I were a good writer," they think, "I wouldn't have to make changes—I'd write it perfectly from the start." They think that revising is a sign of a bad writer.

But in reality, it's the other way around. If you remember nothing else from this book, please remember this: WRITING *IS* REVISING. Even the best, most experienced writers don't get it right the first time. In fact, the more experience a writer has, the more drafts he tends to write. Experienced writers know that they should *first* get their ideas down—however roughly—and *then* worry about making them sound "perfect."

So give yourself the freedom to write rough (really *rough*) drafts. Your goal should always be first and foremost to get your ideas written down. After that, you can refine your organization, word choice, and grammar. Don't worry so much about grammar and spelling that you lose sight of the ideas you need to convey. Instead, keep in mind the following order of priorities:

> ### Writing IS Revising
> A good writer doesn't try to get it right the first time. She tries to get it right the second or third—or even tenth—time. A good writer knows that she needs to get her ideas down on paper where she can see them first. Then she can refine what she's written until it expresses *exactly* what she wants to say, exactly *how* she wants to say it.

1. **Content**—*what you have to say.* Get your ideas out first!

2. **Organization and style**—*how you say it.* Put those ideas into a logical order and in crisp, clear sentences.

3. **Grammar and mechanics**—*the rules for saying it right.* Make sure that what you say is in the right format and that your punctuation and mechanics are correct. A misplaced comma can mean a misunderstood message.

If at any point in this program you find yourself frustrated, come back to this introduction and remind yourself of these basics about the writing process. Meanwhile, write well!

IN SHORT

To be a good writer, you have to be willing to revise, and often. You can find out what needs revising by reading your own work out loud and by getting others to read your work and give you feedback.

Skill Building Until Next Time

Write something. It doesn't matter what, so long as it's something you can write right now: a letter to your mother, a request for a magazine subscription, a memo telling your boss what kind of changes would make your work area a more pleasant place. Don't worry too much about the details. For now, just write. You're getting warmed up for the *real* work ahead.

SECTION 1

THE BASICS OF WRITING FOR WORK

Most of us aren't trained as professional writers, yet most of us have to do some kind of writing at work in the form of reports, letters, memos, evaluations, and the like. Sometimes writing for work can be an intimidating task, especially for those of us who haven't been schooled in the rules of work-related writing. Like writing for the stage or screen, writing for work should follow a specific set of rules and conventions. It demands communication that is logical, clear, and concise.

The chapters in this section are designed to give you a solid understanding of what it takes to write well for work—exactly how to write logically, clearly, and concisely in work-related situations. Specifically, you'll learn:

- What makes writing for work different from other kinds of writing
- How to clearly state your main idea in a workplace communication
- How to offer strong support for your main idea
- How to effectively organize supporting ideas

Did you read the first chapter of this book? If you didn't, please go back and read that chapter before you go on with this section.

CHAPTER | 2

Workplace writing has several characteristics and conventions that make it different from other kinds of writing. This chapter will show you what those differences are as well as how to prepare for any workplace writing task.

WHAT IS WORKPLACE WRITING?

"The writer must therefore constantly ask himself: What am I trying to say? … Then he must look at what he has written and ask: Have I said it?"

William Zinsser

Why do I need a book about workplace writing? Writing is writing is writing. Right? Well, not quite. There are actually many different kinds, or *genres,* of writing, and each genre has its own unique characteristics and conventions (customs or practices) that distinguish it from other genres. Poetry, for example, is as different from biography as novels are from newspapers. Writing in the workplace is no exception, and a big part of becoming a successful writer at work (or in any genre, for that matter) is mastering these characteristics and conventions.

Genres are usually distinguished by a combination of the following five elements:

- subject matter
- audience
- purpose
- format
- style

Let's begin by exploring the nature of each of these elements in workplace writing.

ELEMENTS OF WORKPLACE WRITING

Subject Matter

With few exceptions, the subject of a business communication is exactly that: *business*. Though both the writer and reader may be concerned about more personal or global issues, when it comes down to it, writing *for* work must also be writing *about* work. It's that simple. Any global or personal concerns should be clearly related to the business at hand.

Audience

More than any other kind of writing, workplace writing is audience specific: *What you say and how you say it depends entirely upon whom you are saying it to.* This means that before you begin to write, you need to be very clear about your audience. Who will read your document? Why? What special needs or characteristics does this reader or group of readers have?

> **Audience**
> What you say and how you say it depends entirely upon whom you are saying it to.

Much of what you read outside the workplace is meant for a general audience. Novels, for example, are usually written for a "general reader." These readers typically don't have a special characteristic that enables them to understand or be interested in the material. Their desires, backgrounds, knowledge, opinions, and experiences can be as varied as the colors of the spectrum.

The readers of a workplace communication, however, are always a specific, targeted audience. It may be one person or many, but it should always be an audience that has a definite work-related reason for reading that communication.

Purpose

Workplace writing is also distinguished from other genres by its focus on purpose. In anything you write for work, your reason for writing must be clear from the beginning. In business, as they say, time is money, so your readers don't have the time to read between the lines or play guessing games about your purpose. You must let your readers know, as quickly and as clearly as possible, why you're writing and what it is you want to convey.

This means that before you begin to write, you need to be *absolutely clear* about your purpose. What is it that your communication should accomplish? What exactly do you want to convey? And why? What should happen as a result of what you've written? You'll learn strategies for clearly expressing your purpose in the next chapter.

Format

Just about anything you'll write for work will fall into a few basic formats, which have some specific rules for presentation. Memos, for example, should be set up a certain way, and letters have specific sections that should be arranged in a specific order. While formatting is generally one of the easier parts of workplace writing, it's important to understand why these formats exist, so you can use these conventions effectively. The most common workplace writing formats are discussed in Section 3.

Style

Workplace communications are also characterized by a specific style. When you write for work, you need to be as clear, concise, and straightforward as possible. Remember, time is money, so there's no room for extra or unnecessary words, no time to waste on excessive description or flowery language. A busy manager is not likely to read what you write if you don't get straight to the point. A document full of wordy sentences wastes your reader's precious time and shows a lack of respect for your reader. You'll learn more about how to write clearly and concisely in Section 4.

BEFORE YOU BEGIN

Just as it's not wise to go for a run without stretching, you shouldn't pick up a pen and start writing for work until you've limbered up for your writing task. The best way to do this is to make sure you clearly understand both your audience and your purpose.

Prewriting

Writers often "stretch" by *prewriting*. They brainstorm about their writing task, jotting down ideas about what they want to say and how they want to say it. Some people get started by creating a list of ideas to work with. This is often very effective. But before you create your list, it's important to answer a series of specific questions about your communication. By answering these prewriting questions, you can pinpoint your audience and purpose *before* you begin writing. This makes every stage of your writing process more effective.

Prewriting Questions

1. *Who will definitely read this communication?* (Who is your primary audience?)
2. *Who else might read this communication?* (Who is your secondary audience?)
3. *What should this communication do? What is its purpose?* To answer this question, determine the verb that best describes the **action** of your message. Then name the **object** of that action (the *what*) and/or the **receiver** of that action (the *who*). For example, your purpose might be *to explain* (the action) the *new policy* (the object of that action) to *employees* (the receiver of that action).

Purpose	Action	Object of That Action	Receiver of That Action
welcome the new employees	to welcome		the new employees
explain the new policy	to explain	the new policy	employees
report a violation of procedures	to report	violation	management

Here are some verbs you might use to describe your purpose:

inform	congratulate	offer
convince	claim	explain
report	compromise	describe
review	reprimand	approve
warn	welcome	reject
praise	pacify	demonstrate
summarize	impress	
sell	urge	
propose	demand	
request	correct	
suggest	mediate	
remind	show	

4. *What information must this communication include?* (Don't worry about the order this information should be presented in; for now, just worry about what needs to be said.)
5. *What additional information could this communication include?*

By answering these prewriting questions, you can help ensure that your communication does exactly what it's supposed to do and that its message will be right for your audience. Of course, answering these prewriting questions means investing a little more time up front. But if you answer these questions carefully, you're likely to cut down considerably on revising time later. You'll also write something that effectively achieves its purpose. Knowing what you want to say, to whom, and why is the first step to writing well at work.

PRACTICE

Below are four writing-for-work scenarios. Apply these scenarios to your current job and then answer the prewriting questions for each. The first scenario has been completed as an example. (Note: There is no one right answer for these exercises. Sample answers are provided.)

Sample Scenario Your office received 40 boxes of the wrong paper, and you have to write to your office supply company about the mistake.

a. *Who will definitely read this communication?* Someone at the supply company—probably a customer service representative.

b. *Who else might read this communication?*
  • a manager at the supply company
  • my manager
  • a receptionist or secretary at the supply company

c. *What should this communication do?*
  • report the shipping error to the company
  • restate the original order
  • request that the original order be rush delivered

d. *What information must this communication include?*
  • the original order (item, amount, and date of order)
  • what I received instead (item, amount, date of receipt)
  • how soon I need the correct order

e. *What additional information could this communication include?*
  • any information about my company's relationship with the supplier (e.g., we've never had trouble in the past)
  • a hope that it doesn't happen again
  • any inconvenience the error caused

Scenario 1. Your department has instituted a new dress code/uniform policy, and you have to write a memo explaining the new policy to employees in your department.

a. _____

b. _____

c. _____

d. _____

e. _____

Scenario 2. You are a manager and your newest entry-level employee (line worker, dishwasher, office assistant, etc.) is up for a three-month review. Your boss has asked you to prepare a memo reviewing that employee's performance.

a. _____

b. _____

c. _____

d. _____

e. _____

Scenario 3. Your production group's equipment is old and breaks down frequently. You want to replace everything with new equipment.

a. _____

b. _____

c. _____

d. _____

e. _____

Possible Answers for Practice Exercises

1. a. All employees in my department
   b. My boss, someone in human resources or upper level management
   c. Inform employees about the new dress code
   d. The specifics of the new dress code:
   • what exactly people are required to wear
   • what is and isn't permissible
   • when it goes into effect
   • what penalties people will face for not obeying the dress code
   e. How it's different from the old dress code and why it's been changed

2. **a.** My boss
   b. The employee under review, someone from human resources
   c. Report on this employee's performance
   d. My opinion about how the employee has been performing, specifying his or her strengths and weaknesses
   e. Specific examples of the employee's strengths and weaknesses; suggestions I have about how his or her performance could improve

3. **a.** My manager
   b. Others in charge of budgeting and accounting, other managers
   c. To convince my manager and anyone else involved in the decision-making process to purchase new equipment for us
   d. I must include:
   - what the machines are
   - how often they break down
   - how they slow down production
   - how new equipment could increase production
   - specific information about the new machines we want
   e. How frequent breakdowns affect employee motivation and morale

IN SHORT

Workplace writing differs from other genres in several ways, including subject matter, audience, purpose, format, and style. What you write for work will be most effective if you have a clear understanding of exactly who your audience is, what you want to say to that audience, and why. Brainstorming and answering specific prewriting questions before you begin to write will help you clearly establish your audience and purpose. You will also be able to clarify exactly what information your communication needs to convey.

Skill Building Until Next Time

Take the most recent communication you received at work and move backwards. By looking carefully at how it is written and what it says, can you answer the prewriting questions?

CHAPTER | 3

An important feature of workplace writing is that it always tells the reader *from the beginning* what it's about and why it has been written. This chapter will show you how to clarify your main idea and express it clearly for your readers.

CLEARLY STATING YOUR MAIN IDEA

"The chief aim of the writer is to be understood."

John Dryden

When you pick up the phone to call a friend, or when you stop someone in the hallway or on the street, it's for a reason: You have something to say to that person. Each communication has its purpose.

But while you can chat with a friend for minutes or even hours before you get to the main reason for your call ("I need to borrow your car tomorrow morning"), there's no room for small talk when you're writing for work. The longer you wait to tell your reader why you're writing, the more you risk losing your reader's attention—which means you risk losing your opportunity to convey your message. That's why the beginning of everything you write for work should clearly state its main idea.

MAIN IDEA OVERVIEW

The main idea of a piece of writing is different from its subject and inseparable from its purpose. If your friend calls you and wants to talk about the weather (the **subject**), you'll expect your friend to say something *about* the weather (the **main idea**: "Watch out. There's going to be a big storm today"). The main idea thus reflects the writer's *purpose:* to warn you about the storm.

Subject: who or what the passage is about (for example, the weather)

Main idea: what you want to say *about* that subject (for example, "Watch out. There's going to be a big storm today.")

The main idea, in other words, is usually some kind of *assertion* about the subject—what you think or feel or know *about* that topic. An assertion is also something that requires *"evidence"* or "proof" to be accepted as true. Thus, if your friend tells you that there is going to be a big storm today (an assertion), he should also offer some evidence—"I just heard it on the radio and the sky is already pitch black." The more evidence your friend offers, the more valid his assertion. (Of course, you probably trust your friend to give you accurate information. But in business writing, no matter how credible or trustworthy the source, you should always provide evidence for your assertions.)

> **Main Idea**
>
> The main idea of a text is both an assertion about the subject and an idea that is general enough to hold the whole passage together.

The main idea of a passage is an assertion about its subject, but it is also something more: It is the idea that holds together or controls what you're writing. The other sentences and ideas in what you write should all relate to your main idea. You might think of the main idea as a "net" that is cast over the other sentences; it is a *general* assertion about the topic, and the rest of what you write should offer *specific* support for that assertion. (You'll learn how to provide that support in the next chapter.) Thus, the main idea of a passage is:

- An assertion about the subject
- The general idea that controls or holds together what you write

Here's an example of a main idea that is a *general* assertion:

Subject: Our current office supplies vendor
Main idea: Our current office supplies vendor *is overcharging us.*

Notice that the main idea is *general;* it doesn't provide specific examples or evidence to prove the assertion it makes. That's the work of the rest of the passage, which should provide specific supporting evidence or examples for that assertion. The complete passage might include the following ideas:

Main idea: Our current office supplies vendor is overcharging us.

1. Support: Overcharging $2.00 per ream of paper
2. Support: Overcharging $1.00 per box of envelopes
3. Support: Overcharging an average of $73.00 per shipment for shipping and handling

An assertion can be a **matter of fact**—something that can be objectively and systematically proven to be true, such as "A cheeseburger *costs more* than a hamburger." An assertion can also be a **matter of opinion**—something that is a personal and subjective truth that cannot be verified, such as "Cheeseburgers *taste better* than hamburgers." What about people who dislike cheese? In either case, both assertions say something *about* the subject (cheeseburgers and hamburgers).

The sentence that expresses the general assertion about the subject (the main idea) is often called a **topic sentence** (also called *thesis statement* or *statement of purpose*).

Assertion-Support Structure

Because it's so important to get right to the point in business communications, most paragraphs will begin with a topic sentence which states the main idea of that paragraph. The remaining sentences in the paragraph then support that main idea. Thus, most paragraphs follow a very basic and effective structure: assertion → support. For example, you could write a paragraph like the following:

People who work for themselves are very lucky. They have more freedom than people who work for someone else. They also have more flexibility.

The main idea is expressed in the topic sentence that begins the paragraph, and in workplace writing that's generally the best place for it. Notice also how the second and third sentences provide support for the topic sentence. Thus you have a simple assertion-support paragraph.

But you might also notice that each of the supporting sentences *are themselves assertions* that could use further support. So you could expand this single paragraph into several paragraphs—and you *should,* if you want your message to be more convincing. In this case, the topic sentence of the original paragraph becomes the topic sentence controlling *all three* paragraphs—the main idea for the entire text. The original supporting assertions then become their own topic sentences, in their own paragraphs, requiring their own support:

overall main idea → People who work for themselves are very lucky. They have two main advantages over people who work for others.

main idea for supporting paragraph 1 → First, they're their own boss, which means they have more freedom. They can set their own schedules; they can choose their own projects; and they only have to answer to themselves. } *supporting ideas* They're free to take risks or play it safe, to work all night or sleep all day, and to work in a suit or in jeans and a t-shirt.

main idea for supporting paragraph 2 → People who work for themselves also have more flexibility. They can take on a variety of projects, and they often get to assume a variety of roles. If a family emergency arises, they can handle it with much more ease than someone who works in an office } *supporting ideas* or factory. They can also schedule vacations, doctor visits, and so on with greater ease than someone who works 9–5.

Notice how each individual paragraph follows the assertion → support formula, and how each paragraph also supports the main idea of the entire passage. Of course, the main idea of this passage is a **matter of opinion**. You could just as easily write something with an opposite main idea:

People who work for themselves have many problems and wor-
ries that people who work for someone else don't.

Matters of Opinion

In Chapter 2, you answered prewriting questions for a review of your newest
employee. It's clear what this communication will be about (your employee's
performance); what you need to decide is what you want to say *about* your
employee's performance. What do you **think** or **feel** about it? What is the
main idea that you need to express in a topic sentence?

Your employee might be very prompt, but "Angelo Martinez is very
prompt" would not be a very good topic sentence because it is too specific;
it is only about one of the characteristics that makes Mr. Martinez a good
employee. Unless all you are going to write about is Mr. Martinez's prompt-
ness, this sentence is not general enough for a main idea.

To write a good topic sentence, you need to keep your purpose clearly
in your mind. After all, your purpose determines what you need to say. So
ask yourself why you're writing.

Are you writing:

- To praise the employee for work well done?
- To report that the employee's work is average and to suggest that he
  or she get further training?
- To complain that your employee's performance is not up to par and
  suggest that he or she be replaced as soon as possible?

If you can clearly establish your purpose, then it becomes easy to form
a sentence that clearly expresses your main idea. Your main idea will immediately inform your reader what you *think* or how you *feel* about your subject. And it won't be too specific. Then your reader will also know what to
expect in the rest of your communication: support for your claim (why you
think what you do about this employee). Here's an example:

Purpose:	to praise Ms. Calamari for being an excellent assistant
Topic sentence:	I'm happy to report that Ms. Calamari has proven to be an excellent assistant.
Readers expect:	to see evidence that Ms. Calamari is an excellent assistant

Matters of Fact

Topic sentences for matters of fact are slightly different from topic sentences for matters of opinion. In these situations, what you think or feel about the subject is not what's important but rather **what you know** about it or **why it's important** to the reader. A topic sentence that is a matter of fact is something that can be objectively proven to be true. It is not an opinion about something. But factual topic sentences are still formed the same way as opinion topic sentences and still express something about the subject. Here's an example:

Subject:	new uniform policy
Audience:	all employees in production department
Purpose:	inform employees about the new uniform policy and when it begins
Topic sentence:	A new dress code for all employees will go into effect beginning on the first of the month.
Readers expect:	to hear details about this new dress code

This topic sentence is clear but general—there's still plenty of room for specific supporting paragraphs to describe this policy in detail, which is what readers expect the following paragraphs to do.

PRACTICE

Keeping in mind your audience and purpose, write clear topic sentences for the following writing situations. Remember, there's no one right answer for these questions.

Example:

    Topic: email monitoring

    Audience: president

    Purpose: suggest that employees be notified that email messages may be monitored (matter of opinion)

Topic sentence: Employees should be made aware that any message they send via email may be monitored by the company.

1. *Topic:*   annual Employee Satisfaction Survey

   Audience: all employees

   Purpose: persuade employees to fill out the survey (matter of opinion)

Topic sentence:

2. *Topic:*   recent employee accident

   Audience: safety manager

   Purpose: to explain what caused the accident (matter of fact)

Topic sentence:

3. *Topic:*   changes in the tuition reimbursement policy

   Audience: all full-time employees

   Purpose: to inform them of changes in the tuition reimbursement policy (matter of fact)

Topic sentence:

4. *Topic:*   new automatic time sheets
   Audience: payroll manager
   Purpose: to evaluate the usefulness of the new time
          sheets (matter of opinion)

Topic sentence:

Possible Answers for Practice Exercises

1. It is important that you fill out the annual Employee Satisfaction Survey.
2. Tuesday's accident on the production floor was caused by violation of safety procedures.
3. There have been several changes to the tuition reimbursement policy.
4. The new automatic time sheets make submitting time sheets much easier.

IN SHORT

Whenever you write something at work, you should clearly express your main idea in a topic sentence at the beginning of the first paragraph. Then, readers will know right away not only what your communication is about, but also what you want to say about that subject. Whether your main idea is a matter of opinion or a matter of fact, it should be stated clearly. It should also be general enough to encompass all of the specific supporting ideas that follow it.

Skill Building Until Next Time

As you go throughout your day, choose various subjects and form topic sentences about them. Your subjects can be anything—your work area, your car, or the weather. Form general topic sentences for which you can provide sufficient "evidence."

CHAPTER | 4

If you want what you write for work to have maximum impact, you need to provide strong support for your main idea. This chapter will give you several strategies for providing that support and for organizing your supporting ideas.

CLEARLY SUPPORTING YOUR MAIN IDEA

"The old adage tells us to think before we speak. We should also think before we write. Actually, we should think before we write, while we write, and after we write. Thinking is what the writing process is all about."

Kevin J. Harty

Sam Maplewood wants a raise. He walks into his boss's office, says "I think I deserve a raise," and walks out. Ella Sanders also wants a raise. She walks into her boss's office and says: "I think I deserve a raise. I've been a reliable employee for three years; I've never missed a day of work; I have excellent evaluations; and I came up with the idea for the employee awards, which have boosted morale and increased production."

Ella is more likely to get a positive response than Sam, of course, because she's **supported** her request with reasons why she deserves a raise. The need for specific support seems obvious from the example above, but what seems so clear here is something that people often forget when it comes down to actually writing.

Whenever you're writing for work, if you want your main idea to be taken seriously, you need to support what you say. This support can come from one or more of the following:

- details
- reasons
- examples
- results
- definitions
- comparisons
- quotations or expert opinion
- statistics
- descriptions
- anecdotes (experiences)
- other types of support or evidence

SUPPORT FOR MATTERS OF FACT

Support for matters of fact can come from a variety of sources. You saw one example of a matter of fact in Chapter 2 when you wrote a topic sentence to inform all employees about the changes in the tuition reimbursement program. Your topic sentence might have looked something like this:

> There have been several changes to the tuition reimbursement program.

If you were to write a complete memo, what kind of support would you offer for this statement of fact? The most important thing for you to do is explain *how* the program has changed. So, first and foremost, you must provide:

Details: What exactly are the changes?

If you tell your readers how the program has changed, then you've covered the most important information. Good writers, however, think carefully about their readers' needs. In this case, your readers may also want to know *why* those changes have been made and *how* they will be affected by those changes. Readers also like clear comparisons—they don't want to have to look up a detail from the old policy to see how the new policy is different. Thus, a strong memo would also offer support in the form of:

Reasons:	Why have these changes been made?
Examples:	What might this mean in practical terms for the average employee?
Comparisons:	How does this compare to the old program?

There are many ways to organize this information. One logical approach would be to explain a change, offer the reason for that change, provide a specific example, and offer a comparison (though not necessarily in that order), and then move on to the next change. Thus the support for the main idea is provided by the details (the changes), and each detail (each change) is supported by reasons, examples, and comparisons, giving readers three strong supporting paragraphs. Here's an outline of this approach:

1. Detail: Change 1
   a. Reason
   b. Example
   c. Comparison

2. Detail: Change 2
   d. Reason
   e. Example
   f. Comparison

3. Detail: Change 3
   g. Reason
   h. Example
   i. Comparison

Assume that the three changes in the tuition reimbursement policy are in the following areas:

1. *When* you must apply for reimbursement
2. *How much* you will be reimbursed
3. *How* you will be reimbursed

According to this outline, here's how one paragraph might look:

detail—
the change—
and the paragraph's
topic sentence

comparison

reason

example

> To receive tuition reimbursement, you must now apply for reimbursement at least two weeks before you register for the class. In the past, it was possible to apply for reimbursement up until the end of the semester, but this enabled employees to register for non–work-related classes that cannot be reimbursed under company policy. Thus, if you wish to register on September 1st, you must now submit your application for reimbursement no later than August 17th.

PRACTICE A

Make up specific comparisons, reasons, and examples to write a supporting paragraph for either change 2 or 3 listed above. Start with a topic sentence that clearly explains the change. Some possible changes might be: reimbursement at 80 percent of cost rather than 100 percent; reimbursement only for work-related courses rather than all courses; reimbursement in a separate check rather than in the paycheck; etc. Or you can choose your own changes. The details you provide are up to you. Take out a separate piece of paper and write your sample paragraphs.

SUPPORT FOR MATTERS OF OPINION

To show how to support matters of opinion, let's return to the review of your newest employee. You may have come up with a topic sentence like:

> I'm happy to report that Adrian has proven to be an excellent sorting machine operator.

Now you need to support this assertion. You can use reasons, details, examples, results, comparisons, descriptions, and anecdotes. To make the writing task easier, you might start by first listing the characteristics about Adrian that make him an excellent employee. This is a form of brainstorming. Your list might look something like this:

1. He works well with others.
2. He completes his reports promptly and thoroughly.
3. He regularly meets or exceeds his individual production goals.

4. He volunteers to help others.

5. He is a quick learner.

These five items provide specific support for your assertion—support that's necessary if your assertion is to carry any weight.

But these five supporting ideas are really only a start. As you can see, each of these ideas is also an assertion, and for your review to have *real* impact, you should *support each of these assertions as well.* That is, you should offer specific evidence for each of these supports to *show* that Adrian is a good sorting machine operator.

So, for example, saying that Adrian is a quick learner is evidence that he is an excellent employee. Now you should *show* that Adrian is a quick learner by providing specific examples of that characteristic:

One of Adrian's strengths is that he is a quick learner. Our former sorting machine operator took a week to train; Adrian was ready to begin after just two days even though he'd had no previous line experience. In addition, when Quincy Epstein had an emergency, Adrian volunteered to cover his shift and learned Epstein's line routine in just a few minutes. And when I gave him the machine manual to review, he memorized all the troubleshooting procedures by the end of the week.

main idea for this paragraph

support

support

support

PRACTICE B

Choose from the list of characteristics that make Adrian an excellent sorting machine operator. (You can change Adrian's position to something you're more familiar with, if you like.) Then take out a separate sheet of paper and write another supporting paragraph. Start with a topic sentence and add specific support for that assertion.

PRACTICE C

List three supporting ideas for each of the matter-of-opinion main ideas listed below:

1. Our new health care plan is a big improvement over the old one.

    _____

    _____

    _____

2. The proposed uniform policy will create a better atmosphere at work.

    _____

    _____

    _____

3. We should order machines from Caldecott instead of Apex.

    _____

    _____

    _____

Possible Answers for Practice Exercises

Practice A: Supporting paragraph for change #2

Under the new policy, you will be reimbursed for 80 percent of tuition costs for courses in which you earn a C average or better. Thus, if you pay $1,000 for a course, you will be reimbursed in the amount of $800. This reduction is one of the 30 budget-tightening initiatives passed by the Board of Trustees.

Practice B: Supporting paragraph for characteristic #3

If Adrian is a sorting machine operator: Adrian regularly meets or exceeds production goals. He works steadily and swiftly throughout the day. He won't take lunch until he's hit the halfway mark. He is the top producer in his group with an average of 20 units over goal each week.

If Marcelle Dubois is a custodian: Marcelle does her work efficiently and effectively. Many times Marcelle has finished her cleaning rounds early enough to help others or to work on backlogged projects. She works quickly but thoroughly; I've checked several times and found she cleaned not only to standard, but above standard.

PRACTICE C

The new health plan is a big improvement over the old one:

1. There is only a $200 deductible rather than $400.
2. We can use any doctor; we aren't restricted in whom we can choose.
3. Eye care and dental care are covered under this plan; they weren't included in the old one.

The proposed uniform policy will create a better atmosphere at work.

1. Employees will feel part of a team.
2. Employees will appear—and feel—more professional.
3. Employees will not have to worry about whether or not their clothing is appropriate or stylish.
4. Employees will feel as if everyone is equal.

We should order machines from Caldecott instead of Apex.

1. Caldecott machines are faster.
2. Caldecott offers a better warranty.
3. Caldecott machines cost less.
4. Caldecott offers free on-site maintenance for two years.

IN SHORT

Support for main ideas—whether they're matters of fact or matters of opinion—can come from a number of sources. Use details, reasons, comparisons, examples and more to show readers that your assertions are valid.

Skill Building Until Next Time

Make assertions as you go through your day and provide supporting ideas for them. Your assertions can be about anything—from "I have a really great job" to "Ray's Place has the best pizza in town"—and your support should show how or why that assertion is valid.

CHAPTER | 5

When you write for work, it's important that your ideas are arranged logically. This chapter discusses the major organizing strategies and types of transitions that you can use to organize your ideas.

ORGANIZING YOUR IDEAS

"Good order is the foundation of all good things."

Edmund Burke

Imagine that you've just bought your first automatic coffee machine. Inside the box are instructions that look like this:

1. Place the filter in the brown filter basket.
2. Rinse the coffee pot after use.
3. Pour water in the top vent.
4. Plug in the coffee maker.
5. Place measured coffee grinds in the filter.
6. Press the "on" button, located at the base of the machine.
7. Fill the pot with water. USE COLD WATER ONLY.

Notice the cause/effect sequence at work in this paragraph. One by one, the things Thompson did (or did not do) led up to his accident. (Notice also how the first sentence expresses the main idea. It's a good example of a topic sentence.) You can also see that this paragraph uses both cause and effect and chronological sequence as methods of organization.

Whenever you sit down to write about cause and effect, keep in mind that most events have more than one cause and that most actions generate more than one effect. Thompson's accident, for example, was caused by several things working together, not by one item alone.

Practice B

Arrange the following items in cause and effect order:
- Several employees complained.
- The time sheets were misplaced.
- The checks were late.
- The payroll information didn't get input into the system on time.

Spatial

Ideas can be organized according to spatial principles: from top to bottom, from side to side, from inside to outside, and so on.

This organizing principle is particularly useful when you are describing an item or a place. For example, if you were asked to describe the room where Thompson's accident occurred, you could describe it from top to bottom—start with the ceiling, then move to the walls, and end with the floor. Or you could describe the room by halves or sides—what's on the right side of the room (top to bottom or bottom to top) and what's on the left side. In describing an office layout, you might start with the entrance, then move left, then right. The whole idea here is to move around the space or object logically—that is, don't jump around. Notice the difference in these two paragraphs, only one of which is organized logically:

In the center of the office is a giant desk. To the right of the couch is a cabinet. Next to the desk, against the right wall, is a couch. In the back left corner is a bookshelf. Above the couch is a large painting. Along the left wall are several potted plants.

In the center of the office is a giant desk. Next to the desk, against the right wall, is a couch. To the right of the couch is a cabinet. Above the couch is a large painting. Along the left wall are several potted plants. In the back left corner is a bookshelf.

Clearly the first version has no organizing principle; the readers have to jump all around the office as they read the paragraph. The second version, however, moves from the center of the room to the right, to the left, and back. It makes much more sense and is easier to follow.

Practice C

Arrange the following description of a small factory facility in a logical spatial order.

- Behind the lobby is the employee lounge and cafeteria.
- A gravel path leads from the gate to the factory.
- Human Resources and Accounting are to the left of the lobby.
- The production floor is at the rear.
- The entrance opens into a large lobby.
- The factory is surrounded by a tall iron gate.
- The president, vice president, and managers have their offices to the right of the lobby.

Analysis/Classification

Some writers organize ideas according to the parts or functions of an item, idea, or event.

Imagine, for example, that an alien landed in your back yard. How would you describe the alien? One logical thing to do would be to break it down into its parts. You might begin with its head (or heads), then its torso (if it has one), and then its appendages (legs, arms, tentacles, and whatever else may be attached to its body). Similarly, if you had to describe your job, you might break it down into its various parts: As a team leader, for example, you might report to management, direct your team, and work on the line. All of your duties fall into these three categories, which you might describe like this:

As a team leader, I have three main functions: to report to management, to direct my team, and to work on the production line. Each week I meet with management and submit production reports for my team along with individual reports for each team member. I also report any accidents or incidents involving team members as well as any safety hazards in our area.

As a leader, I guide my team each day by reminding them of production goals and checking their progress throughout the day. I also remind them of safety procedures, offer suggestions for greater productivity, and handle any problems that arise between members or with the machinery.

Finally, a large portion of my time is also spent alongside my teammates on the production line. I rotate from task to task to check on the machines and to give team members breaks throughout the day.

PRACTICE D

On a separate sheet of paper, break down the following items into logical parts or functions:

1. Your office building
2. Days of the year
3. Your job

Order of Importance

You can rank supporting ideas from most important to least important, or vice versa.

Let's return again to describing an office. The parts of an office can be organized spatially and analytically, and also by order of importance. For example, you could begin by describing the president's office, then the vice president's, then the junior vice president's, and on down the line to the workstation of the lowest-ranking employee. Or you could begin with the production floor, since that's where the product actually gets made, and move on to the areas that have less and less to do with actual production of the company's product.

When organizing ideas this way, you need to keep in mind what ideas will be most important to your readers and which ideas are most supportive of your main idea. Often, you'll want to start with the least important and move to the most important. This is especially true when you are building an argument, as in the following example:

> Switching to a concentrated cleaner would benefit the company in several ways. First, it would be easier to transport cleaning equipment from job to job. Second, it would increase the availability of storage space, which is badly needed. Third, concentrated cleaners are more cost effective.

Here, the first supporting idea is good; the second is stronger; and the third, cost effectiveness, is the strongest. However, if you aren't building an argument, or if you think readers might not read all of what you've written, you should reverse the order. That way, your most important idea is the first and therefore most likely to be seen by readers. Here's an example:

> Please attend the union meeting on November 21. Delegates will be discussing proposed changes in our earnings and benefits. We will also elect a new secretary and discuss suggestions for a new meeting location.

- Use least-to-most important when you're building an argument.
- Use most-to-least important when readers might not read the entire document.

Notice how this paragraph starts with the most important item on the agenda at the meeting. If this were a least-to-most-important paragraph, attendance at the meeting might not be as close to the beginning of the paragraph. Busy people often don't read beyond the first line or two of a paragraph.

PRACTICE E

Arrange the following ideas in order of importance. You must determine which order (most → least or least → most) is best for the situation.

Topic sentence: Employees in my department have several concerns about the new tuition reimbursement policy.

- It limits the type of courses employees can take.
- It cuts the reimbursement from 100% to just 50%.
- It delays reimbursement until after the completion of the semester, requiring employees to wait several months before they are reimbursed for their expenses.
- It requires a lot more paperwork.

Comparison and Contrast

When you *compare* and *contrast* items, you show the similarities and/or differences between them.

The first step to a good comparison and contrast is to make sure you're using comparable characteristics. You can't, for example, compare the *height* of A to the *weight* of B. Once you have comparable elements for A and B (for example, 1–cost, 2–availability, 3–efficiency), then there are two ways to organize your discussion: the block technique and the point-by-point technique.

Block Technique

The block technique organizes ideas by item (A and B), not characteristics (1, 2, 3). Discuss all of the characteristics of A first (A1, A2, A3) and then discuss all of the characteristics of B (B1, B2, B3). The result is two "blocks"—a block about A, and a block about B.

Point-by-Point Technique

The point-by-point technique organizes by characteristic (1, 2, 3). Discuss both A and B, characteristic by characteristic, so your result is a point-by-point comparison: A1, B1; A2, B2; A3, B3.

Here's an example of each technique in a comparison and contrast of old and new health care plans:

Point-by-point technique:

The new health plan is a big improvement over the old one. The old plan required a $400 deductible; this plan only requires $200. With the old plan, we could only choose from doctors who were within the plan. The new plan lets us choose whomever we like. Finally, the new plan covers both eye and dental care, neither of which were covered by the old plan.

Block technique:

The new health plan is a big improvement over the old one. The old plan required a $400 deductible, and it limited us to doctors within the plan. It didn't include eye care or dental care, either. The new plan, on the other hand, has a deductible of only $200, and we can choose any doctors we like, regardless of whether or not they're part of the plan. It also covers both eye care and dental care.

PRACTICE F

Make a list of three things to compare and contrast between your previous job and your current job. Arrange these items in a compare and contrast format using either the block or point-by-point technique.

1. _____

2. _____

3. _____

Problem/Solution

Another way to organize your ideas is to identify the problem and then offer a solution or solutions. This is a very common and basic format. Here's an example:

> A number of security guards have complained that their new uniforms don't fit comfortably. Would it be possible to bring in a tailor to adjust the uniforms? If the tailor were on premises just one day for measurements, these complaints could be quickly eliminated.

Notice that this paragraph briefly states the problem and then offers a solution. Unlike other formats, which can be flexible, there's little room for change in this structure. The problem must come first so that readers understand what problem the solution solves.

PRACTICE G

On a separate sheet of paper, write a short problem-solution paragraph for something happening at work.

TRANSITIONS

In writing, *transitions* are the words and phrases that move you from one idea to the next. They show the relationship between ideas. Using transitions will help your words flow smoothly, and enable readers to see clearly how your ideas are connected. To see how much we rely on transitions, read the following paragraph:

> Your ideas are organized. You have to make sure they're well connected. Readers can move smoothly from one idea to the next.

It sounds rather choppy, doesn't it? It's a little difficult to follow, too.

The problem is not that the ideas are unclear; it's that the *relationships between the ideas* are unclear. That's because this paragraph lacks transitions.

Notice the difference that transitional words and phrases make in that choppy paragraph above:

> <u>Now that</u> your ideas are organized, you have to make sure they're well connected. <u>Then</u> readers can move smoothly from one idea to the next.

Simply by adding "now that" and "then"—and connecting two of the sentences—you have a much smoother paragraph.

Certain transitional words and phrases are particularly good for certain organizational strategies. When you've organized something chronologically, for example, words like "then," "next," "before," and so on are the most helpful. Below is a list of many transitional words and phrases and the strategies they're most often used for.

Organizing Strategy	Transitional Words and Phrases
order of importance	more importantly, moreover, in addition,furthermore, above all, certainly; first and foremost; first, second, third, etc.;
chronological	then, next, later, before, after, during, while, as, when, afterwards, since, until; first, second, third, etc.
spatial	beside, next to, along, around, above, below, beyond, behind, in front of, under, near
cause and effect	therefore, because, as a result, so, since, thus, consequently, accordingly, hence, then
compare	likewise, similarly, like, in the same way
contrast	on the other hand, however, on the contrary, unlike, but, yet, nevertheless, rather, instead, whereas, although

Other helpful transitional words and phrases include these:

If You Want To	Use These Transitional Words and Phrases
introduce an example	for example, for instance, that is, in other words, in particular, specifically, in fact, first of all
show addition	and, in addition, also, again, moreover, furthermore
show emphasis	indeed, in fact, certainly
acknowledge another point of view	although, though, granted, despite, even though

PRACTICE H

Look at the sentences from Practice B, E, and F. On a separate sheet of paper, rewrite them into paragraphs and use transitional words and phrases to connect your ideas.

Possible Answers for Practice Exercises
Practice A

1. Plug in the coffee maker.
2. Place the filter in the brown filter basket.
3. Place measured coffee grinds in the filter.
4. Fill the pot with water. USE COLD WATER ONLY.
5. Pour water in the top vent.
6. Press the "on" button, located at the base of the machine.
7. Rinse the coffee pot after use.

Practice B

1. The time sheets were misplaced.
2. The payroll information didn't get input into the system on time.
3. The checks were late.
4. Several employees complained.

Practice C

1. The factory is surrounded by a tall iron gate.
2. A gravel path leads from the gate to the factory.
3. The entrance opens into a large lobby.
4. Human Resources and Accounting are to the left of the lobby.
5. The president, vice president, and managers have their offices to the right of the lobby.
6. Behind the lobby is the employee lounge and cafeteria.
7. The production floor is at the rear.

Practice D

1. For your office building, possibilities include: areas of "blue collar" work and areas of "white collar" work; public areas and private offices; production areas and paperwork areas; financial, management, clerical, production, and maintenance areas; and so on.
2. Days of the year: seasons, months, weeks, workdays and vacation days; week days and weekends, and so on.
3. Your job: answers will vary. Perhaps one part of your job is sorting, one part is carrying, and one part is managing inventory.

PRACTICE E

Answers will vary, depending upon what issues are most important to you. Several employees may say their biggest concern is that the reimbursement is cut by half, while their second biggest concern is that they are limited in what courses they can take. Since they're concerned that their complaint may be overlooked, they've started with the most important point first:

1. It cuts the reimbursement from 100% to just 50%.
2. It limits the type of courses employees can take.
3. It delays reimbursement until after the completion of the semester, requiring employees to wait several months before they are reimbursed for their expenses.
4. It requires a lot more paperwork.

PRACTICE F

Answers will vary. You might compare job duties, location, and salary, for example.

PRACTICE G

Answers will vary. Just be sure that your paragraph moves from a clearly stated problem to a clearly stated solution.

PRACTICE H

1. Practice B: **Because** the time sheets were misplaced, the payroll information didn't get input into the system on time. **As a result**, the checks were late, **and** several employees complained.
2. Practice E: **First and foremost**, the new policy cuts the reimbursement from 100% to just 50%. **Second**, it limits the type of courses employees can take. **Third**, it delays reimbursement until after the completion of the semester, requiring employees to wait several months before they are reimbursed for their expenses. **Finally**, it requires a lot more paperwork.
3. Practice F: At my last job, I worked in a copy room crowded with a large reproduction staff and a dozen fax and copy machines. At my new job, **however**, I have a small office next to the copy/fax room where I can do my paperwork in peace and quiet. My previous job compensated me well per hour, **but** I didn't get paid for holidays and I had limited benfits. Now I have a yearly salary **rather than** an hourly wage and have a paid vacation. **But** the biggest difference is in my responsibilities. At my previous job, I had very few responsibilities. I copied or faxed whatever was put in the "in" box and logged out the work I completed. My new job, **on the other hand**, entails a lot more responsibility. Now I supervise a small team of "document managers," and I am responsible for making sure all documents are logged in, logged out, and processed properly.

(Notice that this paragraph is arranged both by the point-by-point comparison and contrast technique and by order of importance [least to most important].)

IN SHORT

There are several organizing strategies you can choose from to arrange your ideas logically. And you will often use more than just one. Be sure to choose an organizational strategy that makes sense and connect your ideas with strong transitional words and phrases so that your reader can move smoothly between ideas.

Skill Building Until Next Time

Take an article from a newspaper or something that was written for work. Circle all the transitional words and phrases you can find. Then see if you can identify the main organizing strategy.

CHAPTER | 6

Effective workplace communication takes more than just knowing common organizational strategies. It also takes knowing how to group ideas and present information in easily digestible units. This chapter shows you strategies for "chunking" your information and making your communications more readable.

READABILITY STRATEGIES

"What's the secret of business writing that succeeds? Make it easy to understand."

Fran Shaw

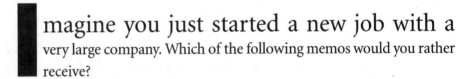magine you just started a new job with a very large company. Which of the following memos would you rather receive?

Memo A:

Please note the locations of the following departments and amenities: Security and Facilities Management is on the first floor. The cafeteria is on the second floor. The employee lounge is located on the fourth floor. The Human Resources and Accounting departments are on the fifth floor. There is a smoking lounge on the sixth floor. Vending machines are on the first, third and fifth floors. The first floor vending machines sell beverages only. The third floor vending machines sell beverages and snacks. The fifth floor machines sell beverages, snacks, and sandwiches.

Memo B:

Please note the locations of the following departments and amenities:

Security and Facilities Management	1st Floor
Cafeteria	2nd Floor
Employee Lounge	4th Floor
Human Resources	5th Floor
Accounting	5th Floor
Smoking Lounge	6th Floor
Vending Machines	1st Floor: Beverages only
	3rd Floor: Beverages and snacks
	5th Floor: Beverages, snacks, and sandwiches

Both memos contain exactly the same information, but Memo B is much more reader friendly. That's because the writer of Memo B used one of several simple **readability strategies** that make information easier to find, follow, and understand. Readability strategies are based on a principle that should drive everything you write: **be reader friendly**. Here are four strategies that will help you be more reader friendly—and help you better organize your ideas as you write:

- Chunk information
- Use headings
- Use lists
- Use tables and graphs

CHUNKING INFORMATION

Good workplace communications divide text into small, manageable units or "chunks" of information. Chunking information follows the same principle as paragraphing. A paragraph is a group of sentences about the same idea. When you chunk information, your aim should be to divide the information into small units of very closely related ideas. If you keep your units small, they become easier to follow, understand, and remember. And if you're thinking about how to chunk your information as you write, you'll end up with paragraphs that are focused and well organized.

To see how this strategy works, let's return to the tuition reimbursement memo you saw in Chapter 4. The main idea "There have been several changes to the tuition reimbursement policy," had the following supporting ideas (the three major changes):

- When to apply for reimbursement
- How much you will be reimbursed
- How you will be reimbursed

These supporting ideas (the changes) were organized *chronologically*. They could also have been organized by order of importance, in which case the second change (how much will be reimbursed) would probably be the most important and therefore the first item in the list. Chronology makes more sense, however, because employees must now apply for reimbursement *before* they register or they won't get reimbursed at all. Then, along with each change, a reason, an example, and a comparison should be provided. Thus, here is the outline for the memo:

Change
- reason
- example
- comparison

In other words, the information was divided into chunks based on each change. The result was the following memo, in which each chunk—the information about each change—became its own paragraph:

The Board of Trustees has voted to implement a new tuition reimbursement program, effective immediately, for Ventura Snacks, Co.

To receive tuition reimbursement, you must now apply for reimbursement at least two weeks before you register for the class. In the past, it was possible to apply for reimbursement up until the end of the semester, but this enabled employees to register for non-work-related classes that cannot be reimbursed under company policy. Thus, if you wish to register on September 1, you must now submit your application for reimbursement no later than August 17.

The new policy also reduces reimbursement from 100% to 80% of tuition costs for courses in which you earn a C average or better. Thus, if you pay $1,000 for a course, and earn a C or higher, you will be reimbursed in the amount of $800. This reduction is one of the "Year 2000 Budget Initiatives" passed by the Board of Trustees.

In addition, you will no longer receive a separate reimbursement check for your tuition. Instead, your reimbursement will be *included in your paycheck* in the pay period following submission of your form. Thus, if your bi-weekly paycheck is typically $1,500, and you requested reimbursement of $800 for a $1,000 course, your next paycheck will be in the amount of $2,300. This revised procedure will save time and money and get you reimbursed more quickly.

This memo is effective; it's well organized and detailed, and it conveys the information employees need to know in small, easy to remember chunks of information. And because each chunk is its own paragraph, with white space (a blank line) both above and below, it's easy for readers to tell where one chunk ends and another begins. In longer documents, of course, chunks may be considerably longer—several paragraphs or even several pages. In that case, reader-friendly writers put extra white space (usually two blank lines instead of just one) between chunks to make the text easier to follow.

HEADINGS

Although this memo is organized, it is not nearly as reader friendly as it could be. Though it chunks information, it doesn't clearly *identify* those chunks of information for readers. That is, readers can't see at a glance what information is contained in each chunk. A quick, easy way to improve this memo is to add **headings**.

Headings are brief titles which indicate the general subject of a paragraph or section. They improve readability dramatically by allowing readers to skim through and identify what kind of information the text contains and where. Headings and **subheadings** (secondary headings) are like a running table of contents; as readers move through the document, they can see the main topic and subtopics of each section. If readers are looking for specific information, they can find it by locating a particular heading. In short, headings and subheadings provide an information "map" for readers. They guide readers through the reading process and help them find, and focus on, precisely the information they need. By breaking up the information, headings also make documents, especially long ones, easier on the eyes and more inviting for the reader.

When you write for work, then, use headings whenever possible. If your document is more than one page long, chances are your information can be broken down into chunks that can be identified by headings.

You can make headings stand out sufficiently against the regular body text by using one of these methods:

- boldface
- underline
- a different font
- a larger font size
- all capitals
- shading

Depending upon the size of your document and the layers of information, you may have several levels of headings. In that case, use one type of heading for all major sections; another, less prominent type for headings of sections *within* those sections; and yet another, less prominent type to indicate your third level of headings. Notice, for example, how the different headings are formatted throughout this book.

Guidelines for Headings

A few guidelines will help you use headings effectively in your workplace communications:

1. **Be consistent.** Use the same font size and style throughout a document so that readers can clearly identify the levels of headings. For example, if you indicate <u>**LEVEL ONE HEADINGS**</u> like this, make sure all level one headings use the same format. Likewise, if you indicate *Level Two Headings* like this, make sure all level two headings are formatted in the same way.

2. **Keep headings brief.** Headings should typically be only a few words long—a short phrase will do. Avoid full sentences. For example, "Filing a Complaint" is a much better heading than "What to Do When You Want to File a Complaint."

3. **Don't get carried away.** You should use headings whenever possible, but that doesn't mean you have to give each paragraph a heading. Remember, headings are your way of guiding readers through your document. Your job is to help them quickly and easily understand your ideas. Too many headings will confuse readers and clutter your document.

Now, notice how much the tuition reimbursement memo improves when headings are added:

NEW TUITION REIMBURSEMENT PROGRAM
The Board of Trustees has voted to implement a new tuition reimbursement program, effective immediately, for Ventura Snacks, Co.

When to Apply
To receive tuition reimbursement, you must now apply for reimbursement at least two weeks before you register for the class. In the past, it was possible to apply for reimbursement up until the end of the semester, but this enabled employees to register for non-work-related classes that cannot be reimbursed under company policy. Thus, if you wish to register on September 1, you must now submit your application for reimbursement no later than August 17.

How Much You Will Be Reimbursed

The new policy also reduces reimbursement from 100% to 80% of tuition costs for courses in which you earn a C average or better. Thus, if you pay $1,000 for a course, and earn a C or higher, you will be reimbursed in the amount of $800. This reduction is one of the "Year 2000 Budget Initiatives" passed by the Board of Trustees.

How You Will Be Reimbursed

You will no longer receive a separate reimbursement check for your tuition. Instead, your reimbursement will be *included in your paycheck* in the pay period following submission of your form. Thus, if your bi-weekly paycheck is typically $1,500, and you requested reimbursement of $800 for a $1,000 course, your next paycheck will be in the amount of $2,300. This revised procedure will save time and money and get you reimbursed more quickly.

With these headings, the chunks—and therefore the organization of the information—are very clear, and at a glance readers can quickly see what types of changes were made to the tuition reimbursement program. This is a much more reader friendly document.

LISTS

Another readability strategy that can help you organize and present your information effectively for your reader is using lists. Lists are reader friendly because they separate items for readers. By organizing information *vertically* rather than *horizontally*, lists allow readers to see each item in the list individually. This makes it easier to digest each idea. Use lists, like headings, whenever possible. If you have three or more items to discuss, consider putting them in a list. Chances are good that a list would make that information easier to follow. For example, notice how the simple sentence below becomes much easier to follow when you put items in a list format:

When entering the construction area, employees must wear the following safety equipment: a hard hat, protective eyeglasses, and a reflective mesh vest.

When entering the construction area, employees must wear the following safety equipment:

- a hard hat
- protective eyeglasses
- a reflective mesh vest

A list makes it much easier to identify each item of protective gear.

The guidelines for effective lists are very similar to the guidelines for effective headings:

1. Use **bullets** to separate items in your list when the items are not in a specific order or priority. Use the same style of bullet for all your bulleted lists throughout the document. Readers may be confused if one list uses •, another uses ➤, and another uses *.
2. Use **numbers** or **letters** of the alphabet to separate the items in your list when you are listing the items in a specific sequence or priority or when there are a specific number of items to remember (for example, "There are three rules for using lists").
3. **Don't overdo it.** Like too many headings, too many lists will distract readers and make your document seem like too many little pieces.

TABLES AND GRAPHS

Tables and graphs organize information **visually** to show the relationship between ideas. They can clarify, simplify, and emphasize information. They're also attractive and often impressive, and sometimes a simple picture can show an idea that might take several paragraphs to explain. When information is complicated (or there's simply lots of it), a table or graph might be used to summarize and reinforce the explanation provided in the text. They're also particularly helpful in conveying information about numbers, especially if you're comparing statistics. Notice, for example, how much more readable Reports B and C are than Report A:

Report A:

Catalog Calls

On Saturday, June 11, we received 110 calls. Fourteen calls (12.7%) were catalog requests; 81 calls (73.6%) were new orders; 5 calls (4.5%) were order adjustments; 6 calls (5.5%) were cancellations; and 4 calls (3.6%) were order status inquiries.

Report B:

Catalog Calls

Below is the catalog call report for Saturday, June 11. A total of 110 calls were received. The vast majority (73.6%) of calls were new orders.

Catalog Calls 6/11/00

Type of Call	Number	Percent
Catalog Requests	14	12.7
New Orders	81	73.6
Adjustments to Orders	5	4.5
Cancelled Orders	6	5.5
Order Status Inquiries	4	3.6
TOTAL:	110	100%

Report C:

Catalog Calls
Below is the catalog call report for Saturday, June 11. A total of 110 calls were received. The vast majority (73.6%) of calls were new orders.

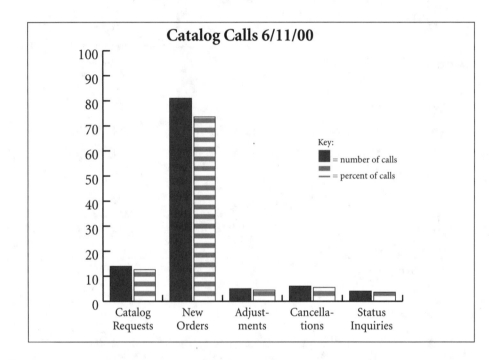

Notice how Report B presents information in a table while Report C presents the information in a graph. In Report B, it's easy to directly compare the numbers. In Report C, the graph makes it easy to visually see the difference in the types of calls. Both reports are far more reader friendly than Report A, which uses regular narrative to tell (rather than show) readers the numbers.

The guidelines for effective tables and graphs are very similar to the guidelines for effective lists and headings:

1. **Use tables and graphs whenever possible and practical**—that is, whenever a visual representation makes more sense than, or is a good supplement to, narrative text. At the same time, however, be careful not to overdo it. While there's no hard rule, unless you're

dealing with a lot of numbers, one large table or graph per page (or two small ones) is probably plenty.

2. **Be consistent**. Use similar formats throughout your document when possible. This makes information easier to compare.

3. Always **introduce tables and graphs** so readers understand exactly what the table or graph is explaining. Use a sentence like "The table below shows…" or "The following graph indicates…"

4. In addition to an introduction, **provide a title** for your table or graph. This way readers can see what the table or graph shows in one quick glance. Notice, for example, how both Reports B and C above introduce the table and bar graph in the first sentence and then provide a title.

Now back to the tuition reimbursement memo. There are other possible ways to chunk the information. Instead of chunking (organizing) by change, you could chunk by the kinds of information in the memo: the changes (one chunk), the example (another chunk), the comparison to the old policy (another chunk), and the reasons (a fourth chunk). The memo would also benefit from each of the three readability strategies discussed in this chapter: clear headings for each section, a list, and a table to visually organize information. Here's the revised memo:

NEW TUITION REIMBURSEMENT PROGRAM
The Board of Trustees has voted to implement a new tuition reimbursement program, effective immediately, for Ventura Snacks, Co.

Major Changes
There are three major changes to the tuition reimbursement policy:

1. You must apply for reimbursement at least two weeks before you register for the class.
2. Reimbursement has been reduced from 100% to 80% of the cost per course.
3. Reimbursement will be included in your paycheck rather than issued as a separate check.

An Example

For example, if you want to register for a course at Tate College, and their registration is on September 1, then you must submit your application for reimbursement to your supervisor no later than August 17. If the course costs $1,000, you will be reimbursed $800, provided you earn a C or better in the course. This $800 will be included in your paycheck two weeks after you submit your reimbursement request form. If your bi-weekly paycheck is $1,500, your next paycheck will be in the amount of $2,300.

A Comparison

The table below summarizes the changes to the tuition reimbursement policy.

Old Policy	New Policy
Apply for reimbursement through the end of the semester	Apply for reimbursement at least two weeks before registration
100% tuition reimbursement	80% tuition reimbursement
Reimbursement issued in a separate paycheck	Reimbursement added to regular bi-weekly paycheck

Rationale

Early application for reimbursement helps ensure that employees are reimbursed only for courses that are relevant to their work. The reduction of reimbursement is part of the Year 2000 Budget Initiatives. Including reimbursement directly in employee's regular paycheck reduces paperwork and processing costs—and gets employees reimbursed more quickly.

If you have any questions about the program, please contact Stacy Williams at extension 443.

This memo is more effective than the previous version for several reasons. First, the information is chunked more effectively. Readers don't have to go through the whole document to find out what the three changes are; that essential information is provided in the first section of the memo.

Second, the information is more effectively organized; each section is much more focused. Third, the list in the first section clearly identifies each change in the program. Fourth, the table in the third section makes it very easy to see the differences in the program by visually setting the old and new policies side by side. In addition, the table neatly summarizes the changes to the tuition reimbursement program.

PRACTICE

Read the memo below carefully. On a separate sheet, rewrite the memo using the readability strategies discussed in this chapter. Divide the information into manageable chunks; provide headings; and use lists, tables, or graphs, if possible, to make the information easier to follow.

A new mandatory drug testing policy will take effect beginning July 1. Under this new policy, all employees will be required to take a urine test four times each year. These tests will be unannounced. Employees who refuse to take the tests will be automatically suspended without pay. This suspension will continue for five days unless they consent to take the test. If they take the test within five days and pass, they will be permitted to return to work as normal, but they will not be refunded for pay lost during the suspension period. Any subsequent refusal will be grounds for dismissal. Employees who do not take the test within the five-day period will be fired. Employees who test positive for substance abuse will face several consequences. To start, they will be immediately suspended without pay. In addition, they must issue a statement explaining how they tested positive for illegal substances. Then, a three-member panel will be assigned to review each employee's case. If an employee has been found to have tested positive due to a legitimate medical condition, he or she will be permitted to return to work immediately and will be reimbursed for the suspension period. If there is no corresponding medical condition, however, the panel has three options. It may recommend that the employee return to work on a probationary basis, with his or her continued employment contingent upon counseling. It may recommend that the employee's suspension continue for a two to four week period.

Or it may recommend that the employee be dismissed. Recommendations will be based upon a careful review of the employee's personnel file, interviews with the employee, and interviews with coworkers. As part of the policy, we have added a professional counselor to our staff, Dr. Nina Long. Dr. Long has extensive experience as a workplace counselor, particularly in dealing with substance abuse. Her office is located in 312B.

Possible Answer To Practice Exercise

There are several ways you could employ readability strategies to make this memo more effective. Here's one way:

NEW MANDATORY DRUG TESTING POLICY

A new mandatory drug testing policy will take effect beginning July 1. Under this new policy, all employees will be required to take a urine test four times each year. These tests will be unannounced.

Refusal to Take the Test

Employees who refuse to take the tests will be automatically suspended without pay. This suspension will continue for five days unless they consent to take the test. If they take the test within five days and pass, they will be permitted to return to work as normal, but they will not be refunded for pay lost during the suspension period. Any subsequent refusal will be grounds for dismissal. Employees who do not take the test within the five-day period will be fired.

Testing Positive

Employees who test positive for substance abuse will face several consequences. To start, they will be immediately suspended without pay. In addition, they must issue a statement explaining how they tested positive for illegal substances. Then, a three-member panel will be assigned to review each employee's case. If an employee has been found to have tested positive due to a legitimate medical condition, he or she will be permitted to return to work immediately and will be reimbursed for the

suspension period. If there is no corresponding medical condition, however, the panel has three options:

1. The panel may recommend that the employee return to
   work on a probationary basis, with his or her continued
   employment contingent upon counseling.
2. The panel may recommend that the employee's suspension
   continue for a two to four week period.
3. The panel may recommend that the employee be dismissed.

Recommendations will be based upon a careful review of the
employee's personnel file, interviews with the employee, and
interviews with coworkers.

Professional Counseling Available
As part of the policy, we have added a professional counselor
to our staff, Dr. Nina Long. Dr. Long has extensive experience
as a workplace counselor, particularly in dealing with substance
abuse. Her office is located in 312B.

IN SHORT

Make your workplace communications reader friendly by dividing your text
into small, easily manageable chunks of information. Guide your readers
by using headings. Make items easy to follow by using lists and present
information visually in tables and graphs.

Skill Building Until Next Time

Notice the way readability strategies are used throughout this book. How
is information divided into small, manageable chunks of information? How
do headings make the chunks easy to follow and show the organization of
the text? How do lists help make information more readable? Finally, when
does the book use tables rather than narrative text to explain ideas and provide information? Why are tables more effective in those situations than
regular sentences or paragraphs?

SECTION 2

GETTING YOUR MESSAGE ACROSS CLEARLY

Although workplace writing may take a variety of forms and cover a wide range of subjects, its function usually falls into one of six major categories:

1. Reporting
2. Asking, acknowledging, or informing: conveying a positive or neutral message
3. Complaining, correcting, or rejecting: conveying a negative or unpleasant message
4. Explaining and instructing
5. Reviewing
6. Convincing

The chapters in this section will show you how to clearly communicate your ideas in each of these six categories.

CHAPTER | 7

Your role as a writer at
work is sometimes much
like that of a newspaper
reporter: you need to
explain what happened,
what you saw, or what
you learned. This chapter
will show you how to
report your findings
effectively and
objectively.

REPORTING

*"[W]riting an effective report depends upon knowing
what the reader wants."*

John C. Brereton & Margaret Mansfield

You probably wrote lots of reports back
in school—and probably didn't expect to be writing so many
once you got to work. Workplace reports aren't really that different from the kind you wrote in school. When you wrote a book report,
you typically summarized the plot and main issues in the novel. In other
words, you gave an account of what you read. And that's what reporting
is all about. *To report,* in fact, is to give an account of something seen, done,
heard, or studied.

At work, you will often be called upon to give an account of something
you've done, seen, heard, or learned. More often than not, you'll have to
put that report into writing.

STRATEGIES FOR WRITING REPORTS

Reports can take several forms, which are discussed further in Section 3. They can also cover a variety of topics. You might write a trip report, an incident report, or meeting minutes, for example. Whatever the type, good reports share the following four characteristics. They're:

1. Accurate
2. Thorough
3. Observant
4. Objective

Be Accurate

In a report, it's essential that you get your facts straight. If you know in advance that you will have to report upon a certain situation, be prepared to take notes. Get a logbook or a notebook in which you can record information and details. Don't simply rely upon your memory; you may not remember key details if you don't bother to write them down. You also may find out later that something you thought was trivial is actually important.

When you write things down, take the time (either at the moment or afterwards) to check that you have spelled names and places accurately and that you have recorded dates, times, and other numbers correctly. If possible, verify any facts about which you are unsure before you submit your report.

In a report, there's no room for guesses. By its very nature, a report is designed to convey facts. From those facts, your readers will draw conclusions, take action, and/or make recommendations. You could be putting your company and your job in jeopardy if you submit a report full of guesses.

PRACTICE A

Record the exact date, time, and location where you are studying this chapter. Be as specific and accurate as possible.

Be Thorough

In any report, there are certain items you must cover: the **who**, **what**, **when**, **where**, **why**, and **how**. These are the basics in any report, and the more specific you can be, the better. Be sure that your report tells readers:

- **Who** was involved?
- In **what**?
- **What** happened?
- **When** did it happen?

- **Where**?
- **Why**?
- **How**?

For example, take a look at the following incident report:

INCIDENT REPORT

Submitted by: <u>Matthew Thomas</u>   Date of Incident: <u>1/21/00</u>
Position: <u>Security Guard, 2nd shift</u> Time of Incident: <u>17 : 18</u>
Date of Report: <u>1/22/00</u>   Location of Incident: <u>Human</u>
                                                 <u>Resources</u>

<u>Description of Incident:</u>
On Monday, January 22, at 16:32, Mr. R. Turner, a former employee, signed in at the security desk. He exchanged his driver's license for a visitor pass and put his destination down as Human Resources. At 17:18, I received a call from Maria Louis, the assistant director of Human Resources. She asked me to come to Human Resources immediately because Mr. Turner refused to leave the office and she could not lock up.

I left Mark Davidson on duty at the desk and reached Human Resources at approximately 17:21. When I arrived, Mr. Turner was sitting by the receptionist's desk. I told Mr. Turner that the office was closed and that he had to leave. He said he would not leave until he saw John Francis, the director of Human Resources. Maria then told me that Mr. Francis was not in that day and that she told Mr. Turner several times that Mr. Francis was not in, but Mr. Turner did not believe her. She said Mr. Turner was waiting because he believed he would catch Mr. Francis as he tried to leave. Then I asked Mr. Turner if this was true, and he said yes. I told him that Mr. Francis was not in and that he could no longer sit in the Human Resources office. If he wished to wait, he could wait by the security desk, but he would be waiting until tomorrow morning. Then I asked Mr. Turner to follow me, and he did.

After I escorted him to the security desk, I asked him if he wanted to wait or if he wanted his ID back. He said he'd come back later, so I returned his ID and he signed out at 17:30. Maria had followed us to the security desk, and after Mr. Turner left, she told me that Mr. Turner had just been fired for failing to pass a random drug test.

Notice that this report is very thorough. It tells readers exactly who was involved, in what, and when, where, why, and how it happened.

Report Questions

A report needs to answer the key questions:

Who, what, where, when, why, how?

PRACTICE B

On a separate sheet of paper, answer the *who, what, when, where, why,* and *how* questions for what you are doing right now or for what you were doing before you started this chapter.

Be Observant

One characteristic that all good reporters have in common is their attention to detail. They're observant; they look closely and listen carefully. When you write a report for work, you, too, need to be observant. A little detail that you notice can make all the difference in how (or how much) you, your company, and/or your coworkers benefit from your report. Details that you can look for include:

size	location
color	temperature
sound	manner
pattern	type or kind
tone	name
shape	brand
texture	material
time	style

The incident report, on page 69, for example, provides several specific details. It tells where Mr. Turner logged in, what ID he used (his driver's license), where he was sitting, and several specific names and times. Here's the first paragraph of the report again with all of the details underlined :

> On <u>Monday</u>, January 22, at <u>16:32</u>, Mr. R. Turner, <u>a former employee</u>, signed in <u>at the security desk</u>. He exchanged his <u>driver's license</u> for a visitor pass and put his destination down as Human Resources. At <u>17:18</u>, I received a call from <u>Maria Louis</u>, the <u>assistant director of Human Resources</u>. She asked me to come to Human Resources immediately because Mr. Turner refused to leave the office and she could not lock up.

Details like these can help in the assessment of an event and serve as important references in the future.

PRACTICE C

The next time you are in your work area, stop and look around very carefully. See if you can write down *at least* a dozen different things you notice about your work space. The more you list, the more you must call on your powers of observation and your eye for detail. You may be surprised at some of the things you take for granted and never really noticed before.

Be Objective

If reporters start to color their articles with their own feelings and impressions, they lose their objectivity and, to a degree, their credibility. As reporters, their job is to provide the facts so that readers can then form their own opinions about the people and circumstances described.

When reporters offer impressions and opinions, their report takes on the status of an analysis, review, or editorial. It can no longer be considered a straight news story or report. Look, for example, at the difference between these two sentences:

1. Mr. Turner said he wouldn't leave until he spoke to Mr. Francis.
2. Mr. Turner is a stubborn jerk.

Sentence 1 tells readers just the facts. Sentence 2, on the other hand, expresses an opinion about Mr. Turner (and not a very nice one at that). Clearly, sentence 2 is not material for a report.

Conclusions or Recommendations

Some types of reports include a section for conclusions or recommendations. If you are writing this kind of report, you should offer conclusions or recommendations that you feel are logical based upon what you've seen, heard, or learned. Clearly the recommendation of a report will be subjective, but in order for it to be valid, it must be based upon the *objective* material presented somewhere in the report. For example, if Mr. Thomas's

Incident Report had a section for recommendations, Mr. Thomas might write something like this:

> Comments/Recommendations:
>
> I recommend that all security staff be notified of this incident and that Mr. Turner not be allowed to enter the building unless he is escorted by Mr. Francis. Ms. Louis was clearly shaken by the incident and said that though Mr. Turner sat quietly, because of the nature of his dismissal, she was concerned for her safety.

PRACTICE D

1. Cross out the sentences (or parts of sentences) that are not objective in the following trip report:

    On Thursday, September 18, I visited the new plant in Smithtown. I traveled by car. The drive, which was pleasant despite the traffic, took three hours. I arrived at 10:00. I met with Floor Manager Jim Martin—a really nice guy—who showed me how the new Quality Control system works. Whoever thought up this system is a genius. Then we had lunch with a line group. Lunch left a lot to be desired but I got to hear how the workers felt about the new system. Each employee had something positive to say about it. I left at 2:00 p.m.

2. Take out a piece of paper and answer the who, what, when, where, why, and how questions for the most recent work "event" for which you were present—a meeting, an incident, an important discussion, or any other noteworthy occurrence. If you can't remember some facts, try to find them out and verify any guesses. Include as much detail as possible in your answers.

3. Go over your answers to question #2. Did any impressions or opinions creep in there? If so, cross them out.

Possible Answers for Practice Exercises

PRACTICE A

Answers will vary. You might have written something like: Friday, June 11, 1997. 8:15 p.m., at the table in my kitchen, in my apartment at 315 Sycamore Lane, Teasdale, RI, USA.

PRACTICE B

Answers will vary. Your answer is a good one if you included detailed responses to the *who, what, when, where, why,* and *how* questions.

PRACTICE C

Answers will vary. You might notice details such as old magazines (how old? what kind?) stacked in a pile, rags in the corner, or the shape, size, and color of bottles some cleaning solutions are stored in. The more specific and detailed your observations, the better.

PRACTICE D

1. On Thursday, September 18, I visited the new plant in Franklintown. I traveled by car. The drive, ~~which was pleasant despite the traffic~~, took three hours. I arrived at 10:00. I met with Floor Manager Jim Martin ~~a really nice guy~~ who showed me how the new Quality Control system works. ~~Whoever thought up this system is a genius~~. Then we had lunch with a line group. ~~Lunch left a lot to be desired~~ but I got to hear how the workers felt about the new system. Each employee had something positive to say about it. I left at 2:00 p.m.

2. Your answers will vary, but here's an example.
   Event: A meeting.
   Who was involved? John, Christine, and I.
   In what? A lunch meeting.
   What happened? We arranged the holiday schedule.
   When? From 1:00–2:20 p.m. on Monday, December 1.
   Where? In the cafeteria.
   How? We each brought our group schedules and time-off requests and charted which shifts needed additional coverage. Then we took the extra shift requests, ranked them by seniority, and put those people in the spots that needed coverage.

Why? To ensure that all shifts are covered during the winter holidays.

3. Note that the above example contains no opinions.

IN SHORT

Reporting is an important function in workplace communications. It requires you to be accurate, thorough, observant, and objective. Use the *who, what, when, where, why,* and *how* questions to get yourself started, and be sure to check the accuracy of your data.

Skill Building Until Next Time

Read through the newspaper and notice the difference between regular articles and those labeled "analysis," "review," or "editorial." All include facts, but some are clearly more objective than others. Notice how a regular report answers the *who, what, when, where, why,* and *how* questions and provides details and specific names, numbers, and facts for readers.

CHAPTER | 8

This chapter deals with a number of everyday tasks your workplace communications may have to fulfill. You'll learn strategies for effectively thanking, requesting, inquiring, and more.

CONVEYING A POSITIVE OR NEUTRAL MESSAGE

"Any institution that won't take the trouble in its writing to be both clear and personal will lose friends, customers, and money."

William Zinsser

Fortunately, a lot of workplace writing involves communicating good news—a much easier task than handing out bad news. Take a look at the following memo as an example:

Dear Reader:

Thank you for purchasing LearningExpress' *Improve Your Writing for Work*. We are pleased that you have chosen our book and are certain that our guide will help you to become a better writer. If you have any comments, please feel free to write us.

We wish you the best of luck as you work through each chapter. Write well!

Sincerely,
LearningExpress

Not only is this letter a sincere thank you; it's also a good example of the kind of writing this chapter is all about: conveying a positive or neutral message in a letter or memo. Specifically, you'll learn about the following kinds of messages in this chapter:

- Informing and reminding
- Requesting and inquiring
- Following up and responding
- Thanking, welcoming, and congratulating

These may seem like a lot of different functions, and they are—but when writing for these purposes, you will use many of the exact same strategies.

THREE BASIC STRATEGIES

Three basic strategies are important for all positive or neutral messages:

1. Clarify your purpose.
2. Choose the proper tone of voice.
3. Provide all the necessary information.

Clarify Your Purpose

The first strategy for writing these kinds of letters and memos should be no surprise: **clarify your purpose and express it in a clear topic sentence.** If you've answered your prewriting questions, this should be an easy task. All you need to do is turn your *purpose* into a *topic sentence*, which you can then use to begin your letter or memo. Here's an example:

purpose:	to congratulate Erik on his recent promotion
topic sentence:	Please accept my warmest congratulations on your recent promotion.

Choose the Proper Tone of Voice

Next, be sure to use the proper tone of voice. This means you need to remember whom you're writing to and use the right kinds of words and "attitude." Are you:

- A superior writing to a subordinate?
- A subordinate writing to a superior?
- A coworker writing to an equal?
- A customer/client writing to a company?
- A company writing to a customer/client?
- A company writing to a potential customer/client? (or vice versa?)

If you're a subordinate writing to a superior, for example, you might write something like:

The manager at my bank needs documentation from my employer regarding my salary and employment history so that I may be approved for a loan. Would you be so kind as to write that letter?

This is a gentle, polite (but not overly polite or flattering) request. A superior writing to a subordinate, on the other hand, would still be polite but be more straightforward or demanding, as in the following example:

Please submit your report no later than Friday at noon.

Whatever your relationship to the reader, one rule always applies: *be human.* Don't try to sound like someone or something you're not. Letters and memos come *from* real people *to* real people, and the tone of voice should always reflect that.

Provide All the Necessary Information

Your tone may be just right and your purpose clear, but you won't get the results you desire if you omit important information. Be sure to brainstorm carefully before you begin so that you don't accidentally leave something out.

Now let's look at some specific functions these letters and memos may serve and how to convey your message effectively for each function.

INFORMING AND REMINDING

The strategies for a communication that aims to inform or remind are really very simple:

1. Tell your readers what you're going to tell them.
2. Tell them.
3. Tell them why you've told them (if appropriate).

In other words,

1. Provide an opening sentence that tells your reader your purpose in a clear, general topic sentence.
2. Provide the specific information you need to convey.
3. Indicate to the reader why this information is important.

Here's an example:

what I'm going to tell them —— There has been a change in the schedule for "Bring Your Daughters to Work Day." There will now be a luncheon for all employees and their children from 12–1:30 p.m. Please let Mickey Andrews know no later than Friday if you will attend. *— telling the*

why I've told them —

The same "tell them" formula applies to reminders. Notice that there are at least three ways to begin the following memo:

what I'm going to tell them —— [We are writing to remind you] [This is a reminder] [Please be reminded] that there will be a meeting with union delegates on Thursday, March 19. The meeting will be held from 4–6 p.m. in the Red Lounge of the Wallace Hotel. Your participation as a union member is important. We will be discussing several issues that may have a significant impact on your future wages and benefits. Come to ask questions and to make your voice heard. Please call Anna Zuchero at 123–4567 if you need directions. We look forward to seeing you at the meeting. *— telling the*

*why I've told them *

PRACTICE A

Use the "tell them" formula to write the following brief message on a separate sheet of paper: a reminder to your supervisor about the dates you've scheduled for your vacation days this year.

REQUESTING AND INQUIRING

Requests and inquiries follow the same general format as communications that inform and remind. Specifically, in requests and inquiries you should:

1. **Tell them what you're going to tell them:** Outline the general nature of your request.
2. **Tell them:** Make the specific request (kindly). Be as detailed as possible so your reader knows exactly what you want.
3. **Tell them why you've told them:** Explain why you need it and by when, if applicable.
4. **Thank them:** Remember that unless you're under contract, no one is obligated to give you anything. People are far more likely to give you what you want if you are gracious about it.

Ordinary Requests

In workplace writing, there are essentially two kinds of requests and inquiries: **ordinary** and **extraordinary**. Ordinary requests are those that fall under normal business circumstances and relationships—a potential customer requesting a brochure, a current customer inquiring about a new service, and so on. In the case of ordinary inquiries and requests, it is essential to be very clear and state exactly what information, product, or service you desire. But it usually is not necessary to explain *why* you want that information, product, or service; it's understood. Take a look at the following example:

Dear Sir/Madam:

I would like a copy of your latest catalog. Please send it to the address listed above at your earliest convenience. Thank you.

This writer doesn't need to explain why she wants the catalog. It's understood that she wants it because she may make a purchase, and companies are usually more than happy to give you standard product/service information in the hope that you will become a customer (or that they will keep you satisfied if you already are a customer).

Extraordinary Requests

However, if you are not a potential or current customer, or if you would like something beyond the normal request or inquiry (an *extraordinary* request), you should explain, in detail, why you want that information, service, or product. After all, normal requests and inquiries have the potential to increase or improve business, so the addressee has a stake in responding positively to your request or inquiry. But this is not the case for special requests like the one in the following example:

> Dear Coworkers:
>
> Time is money—and your time could mean money that's desperately needed for important medical research and services. I'm writing to ask for your time. As you may know, I volunteer at the Children's Hospital. Next month, the hospital is sponsoring a 5K run/walk. Will you participate? We need runners and walkers as well as volunteers to cover registration and t-shirt distribution. The run/walk is on Sunday, May 10, and starts at 9 a.m. If you'd like to participate, please call me at extension 3035. The registration deadline for participation is April 20. Please help us help children.

Notice how this special request lets readers know *why* they're being asked to do something out of the ordinary business routine.

PRACTICE B

On a separate sheet of paper, write a company or organization to request information about a product or service that would be useful to you personally or professionally. Include specific details in your request.

FOLLOWING UP AND RESPONDING

When you've met with someone about a plan or idea, or when someone has requested something from you, you need to *follow up* on that communication. For this type of letter or memo, keep in mind the "tell them" formula we've been using so far and add these rules of thumb:

1. Begin by thanking the person for the letter, memo, telephone call, meeting, etc.
2. Remind the person of the highlights of your meeting or conversation, if applicable. Provide the information or item the person requested, and/or explain why you can't provide it.
3. End on the assumption that you will continue working together or with a "looking forward" or "best wishes" type of statement.

Here's an example:

Kara:
Thanks for your memo about the Children's Hospital run/walk. I'd love to participate. I can run in the race and I'll also be able to help with preparations. I'm free every night but Wednesdays to help. Just let me know what I can do. I'm looking forward to the race and to working for a good cause.

Notice how the memo:

1. Opens with a thank you
2. Provides the information that was requested
3. Ends with a "looking forward" statement

Practice C
On a separate sheet of paper, write a response to the letter you wrote in Practice B.

THANKING, WELCOMING, AND CONGRATULATING
When you write to thank, welcome, or congratulate someone, you're often reiterating something you've already said in person or on the phone. But by sending a written communication, you're showing that your sentiments are sincere enough for you to take the extra time and effort to put it in writing.

For communications that thank, welcome, or congratulate, follow the "tell them" formula, with the following specifications:

1. Be specific about what you're thankful to the person for/welcoming the person to/congratulating the person for. Use exact names, dates, places, and so on.
2. For thank you's, explain briefly why you're grateful—what the person did that deserves special thanks. For congratulations, you might also indicate what a promotion or other achievement means to you. For a welcome, you might indicate how that person's arrival will affect you.
3. Be short, sincere, and on time. If your message is too long, you may come off sounding insincere. And remember that timing is important. Make sure you send your thanks, welcome, or congratulations promptly. A late message may be interpreted as a sign that you don't really mean it.

PRACTICE D

On a separate sheet of paper, write a brief note for one of the following:

1. Thank your boss for recommending you for a promotion (subordinate to superior).
2. Welcome the newest entry-level employee to your workplace (superior to subordinate).
3. Congratulate a coworker on a recent award (coworker to equal).

Possible Answers for Practice Exercises
Practice A

This memo is to remind you of the dates I have selected for vacation this year. I will use four vacation days in August on the 18th, 19th, 22nd, and 23rd and four days in December on the 24th and the 26th–28th. If there is any problem with my selections, please let me know as soon as possible. Thank you.

Practice B

I am interested in purchasing a dozen adjustable workbench stools. Please send me information regarding the type of stools you carry and their prices. Also, please let me know how quickly you would be able to ship the stools should we decide to purchase them from your company. Thank you.

Practice C

Thank you for requesting information about our workbench stools. We are proud of our wide selection and affordable pricing. Our most recent catalog is enclosed. Should you wish to order from us, you can expect to receive shipment within 2–4 weeks for most models. Please let me know if you have any other questions or if I can be of further assistance. I look forward to your order.

Practice D
#2, Letter to welcome new employee

Dear Ms. Swede: [I'd like to welcome you] [Welcome] to our department. I am pleased to have someone with your experience on board. Please let me know if there's anything I can do to help make you comfortable here.

IN SHORT

The general formula for communications about positive or neutral matters is to:

1. Tell your reader your general purpose.
2. Provide specific details.
3. Explain why what you've said is important.

A sincere thank you or good wishes will add a nice touch that will help you get the results you desire.

Skill Building Until Next Time

Think about how you inform, request, thank, and congratulate people in person. Notice that you often follow the "tell them" formula. Listen for this formula as you talk with others.

CHAPTER | 9

Sometimes your work requires you to communicate bad news. This chapter will show you how to convey a negative or unpleasant message—complaining, correcting, or rejecting— in a way that will earn (or maintain) the respect of your reader.

CONVEYING A NEGATIVE OR UNPLEASANT MESSAGE

"He that respects not is not respected."

George Herbert

magine you sent your resume to Ratner's Office Supply in response to a help wanted ad. A week later, you receive the following letter in the mail:

Are you kidding? How could you even *think* we'd hire you? You have no experience in this type of work. Try applying for a job you can actually do next time!

If you ever receive a rejection letter like this, you should be glad you were rejected by the company that sent it! Whoever wrote such a letter has to learn two important rules for writing letters that deliver bad news:

1. Always respect the reader.
2. Always respect the reader.

The rule is worth repeating because it's a rule that should never be broken. When the news you have to convey is not something the reader will want to hear, how you convey it becomes critical to maintaining a positive relationship with the reader. After all, you're writing for work, and you want to keep supervisors, subordinates, customers and potential customers, employees and prospective employees—in short, everybody—as happy as possible, given the circumstances. So bad news has to be delivered tactfully and respectfully in words that show you have given careful thought to the situation. You'll learn how to do that for letters and memos in which you must:

- complain
- correct or adjust
- reject or refuse
- remind or demand

The Most Important Rule

The main rule for writing letters or memos of complaint is "Always respect the reader."

COMPLAINING

The equipment you ordered doesn't work and the customer service representative you spoke with on the phone was rude. This and other situations like it may call for a letter of complaint.

For letters of complaint, follow the "tell them" formula that was discussed in the previous chapter:

- Tell your readers what you're going to tell them.
- Tell them.
- Tell them why you've told them (if appropriate).

When you "tell them," be sure to:

1. Describe the exact product, service, or item you wish to complain about.
2. Describe exactly what is/was wrong with that product, service, or item.

When you "tell them why," you should:

3. Describe any inconvenience the error caused you.
4. Describe exactly what action you want taken to rectify the situation.
5. Request a prompt response to your complaint.

That's the basic formula for writing a good letter of complaint. But these concerns deal only with the content of such a letter. A good letter of complaint also establishes the right tone. Below are some suggestions to help you in this area.

Don't Be Abusive

Keep your emotions in check and don't rant and rave ("Your company stinks! I can't believe you sell this junk!"). With insults and attacks, you will only lose ground, not gain it. Make sure you're calm when you sit down to write.

Some people like to write a version of the complaint that says what they really think. Writing down that version—and then tearing it up—provides the emotional release they need when they're angry. Then they can sit down and write the calm, measured letter they will actually send.

Be Reasonable

Make sure your complaint and the action you would like to be taken match the nature of the problem. For example, don't demand a refund for the full purchase price if you had and used the product for a year before it broke down.

Use "I" Instead of "You"

People tend to be defensive when you hurl a lot of "you"s at them in a letter of complaint. Using "I" and eliminating as many "you"s as possible takes the heat off of your reader so he or she can be less defensive and more objective about your complaint. Notice the difference that eliminating "you" and using "I" makes in the following example:

> **Uses "you":** You didn't send me the parts I ordered on time and you made me miss an important production deadline. You better not let this happen again.

> **Uses "I" and eliminates "you":** The parts I ordered were not shipped on time and as a result I missed an important production deadline. I cannot afford to have this happen again.

Leave the Door Open

Don't burn bridges by refusing to work with the reader(s) ever again. If you do, you're much less likely to get a response to your complaint. After all, why should they bother? You've said you don't want to work with them anymore. Besides, it's dangerous to be absolute. You might come back to them two years down the road because they have a product, service, or skill you need.

Sample Memo of Complaint

Now, let's look at an example of a memo that uses the strategies for content and proper tone in a letter or memo of complaint. The sentences are numbered so you can see each of the "tell them" strategies (see previous page) at work.

TO: Susan Niss
FROM: Fred Gregory
DATE: February 4, 1997
RE: Problems with soap dispensers

(1) My cleaning crew continues to have problems with the soap dispensers recently installed in the bathrooms throughout the hotel. (2) It's nearly impossible to leave the bathrooms clean because the dispensers leak, leaving a soapy mess on the sink counter. (3) As you know, rooms are cleaned between check-out and check-in, but by the time a new guest checks in, there's

already a soapy mess running down the counter into the sink. (3) Needless to say this does not leave a good impression on our guests or management. (4 & 5) Please see what you can do to replace these dispensers as quickly as possible. Thank you.

PRACTICE A

Your paycheck did not include overtime for the third pay period in a row. Using a separate sheet of paper, write a memo of complaint to your accounting department.

CORRECTING AND ADJUSTING

What happens when you're on the other end and you receive a complaint or realize that you've made an error? Much of the same advice applies for answering complaints as for writing them. Stick to the "tell them" format and keep in mind the following strategies:

1. Apologize, but don't be overly apologetic. You don't want to sound insincere or desperate.
2. Be specific about how you will correct or have corrected the problem—or why you can't do anything about it.
3. Be specific about exactly what happened to cause the problem, but don't make empty excuses. If it was actually the complainer's fault, make a suggestion that can help prevent future problems. You could say, "In the future, you may be able to avoid this problem by faxing your order directly to our manufacturer."
4. Avoid absolutes like "This will never happen again." It just might.
5. End on a positive note. For example, remind writers of complaint letters how important their business is, or thank them for pointing out the error.

Responding to Errors

Here are two memos about an error. One follows the guidelines above and the other doesn't. Notice how much more effective the second memo is:

Memo A

I have to confess that the report I submitted last week had an error. I am so, so sorry! You don't know how badly I feel about it. I promise it will never happen again. I was just so over-worked—I had worked a double shift that day—and I didn't have time to check my report over before I submitted it. You know how crazy it gets when we're really busy.

Memo B

I am sorry to report an error in my report of October 3. The total number of units produced was 110, not 141. I made an error in addition. In the future, I will double check my reports for accuracy before I submit them. In the meantime, I'll see what I can do to increase units to 141.

PRACTICE B

You received a memo from an employee complaining that his paycheck did not include overtime for the third pay period in a row. On a separate sheet of paper, respond to this complaint.

REJECTING AND REFUSING

Many people put off writing letters of rejection or refusal because it's not always easy to say "no." But like letters that welcome, congratulate, or thank, letters that reject or refuse need to be sent promptly. If they're not, the discomfort you were trying to avoid on the reader's part will only be compounded with time. There tends to be less sting when a person applying for a job knows within a week that he will not get it. If you wait a month to tell the applicant, you're allowing him to get his hopes up and think "no news is good news." The later your news arrives, the greater his disappointment will be.

The first rule, then, is to *be prompt.* Here are some other tips:

1. Begin by thanking the person for sending her resume, for offering his ideas, etc.

2. State something positive about the person or the situation, if possible. For example, you might write: "We were impressed by your resume," or "I am honored that you have nominated me for the position of Union Delegate."

3. Be firm, but not harsh. For example, a sentence like "Unfortunately, we are unable to offer you a position at this time" is much better than "You didn't get the job." Likewise, "I must refuse the nomination" is better than "Thanks, but no thanks."

4. If appropriate, explain why you are rejecting or refusing the person or the offer. You might say, "We require a candidate with at least one year of experience" or "I have family obligations right now that must take priority."

5. Conclude with an appropriate hope or wish, like "We wish you the best of luck in your job search" or "I am sure that whoever else you nominate will do a fine job representing us."

See how this type of communication works as you read the example pieced together from above (notice the transitions, too):

> I am honored that you have nominated me for the position of union delegate. However, I must refuse the nomination as I have family obligations right now that must take priority. I am sure that whoever else you nominate will do a fine job representing us.

PRACTICE C

Julia Faust applied for a promotion within your department but did not get it. Your boss has asked you to draft a rejection letter to her. Using the tips mentioned above, write the letter on a separate sheet of paper.

REMINDING AND DEMANDING

Occasionally (or often, if you have the pleasure of being a bill collector), you will have to communicate a reminder, warning, or demand. The main rule for this type of communication is that your message must match the nature of the problem. Someone who is 15 days late on a payment or with a report does not deserve a threatening letter or memo. In fact, if that person is normally prompt, all you need is a brief reminder like the following:

February 15, 2000

This is a reminder that annual reviews were due on the 1st of February. We have not yet received your review, which is very important in helping us evaluate your growth as a valuable employee. Please let us know immediately if there is any problem interfering with your completion of this report or if you would like us to send you samples of other annual reviews to help you in this process.

This reminder does two things:

- It stresses the value of the annual review.
- It offers the employee a "way out"—an opportunity to explain why the report isn't done and to get it in without any real penalty.

A second notice, however, needn't be as friendly. Any subsequent notices should begin with a reminder of the employee's obligation. They should also ask if something is preventing him from doing what he is supposed to do—maybe it's not his fault. Finally, your communications should give a deadline of some sort. "Immediately" or "as soon as possible" often works best if the situation is not something absolutely urgent, as in the following example:

March 1, 2000

Your annual review was due on the 1st of February. It is now one month late. If there is a problem preventing you from completing this report, please let us know immediately. Otherwise, we expect you to submit your report as soon as possible.

If, after such a notice, you still don't get the response you desire, your next communication should be less cooperative and more demanding. It's okay to offer a vague threat. If you'd like to offer a specific threat (for example, "If we do not receive payment within 10 days, we will report your delinquency to a collection agency"), make sure it's a threat you can stick to. You should also continue to offer a way out; if you don't, the person may say, "Well, if you're going to send a lawyer after me no matter what, I may as well wait to pay."

PRACTICE D

1. George Reade has been late for work 10 times in the last two weeks. Remind him in a memo (on a separate sheet of paper) that he is expected to be on time and warn him that continued lateness will get him fired.
2. It's two months later, and George Reade continues to be late. It's time to give him a written ultimatum.

Possible Answers for Practice Exercises
Practice A

I am having a serious problem with my paychecks. For the third pay period in a row, my paycheck has not included my overtime pay even though I submitted my time sheets on time. Three weeks ago when the first error occurred, I was told by your office that the missing overtime pay would be included in my next check; it was not, and that check was also missing overtime pay for *that* pay period. The same thing happened the following week. I am now owed three weeks of overtime pay. This error has put me in a difficult financial situation as I depend upon this overtime pay. Please correct the error immediately so that my future checks contain the overtime pay I earn each week. In addition, I expect to receive the overtime pay that is owed to me without any further delay. Please call me at extension 548 to let me know when I can pick up my past-due overtime pay. Thank you for your prompt attention to this matter.

Practice B

We deeply regret the recent error in your paychecks. We have discovered that there was an error in your account on the payroll system and we have corrected the problem. Your future checks should include the overtime pay you are due. We have also prepared a check for the overtime pay that is currently owed to you. You may pick up that check tomorrow morning after 10:00.

Practice C

Thank you for your application for the position of department manager. I am sorry to inform you that you have not been awarded the promotion. Your reviews have been excellent since you joined us six months ago and you have achieved great success in your sales, but we would like you to have at least a full year of sales experience with us before you move into a management position. We sincerely hope that you will apply for this position again next year.

Practice D

1. As an employee of the second shift, your hours of work are 4 P.M.–12 A.M. Your time sheet shows that you have been late 10 times in the past two weeks. Because others depend upon you to complete their work in a timely manner, and as we have an around-the-clock operation, it is important that you arrive promptly at 4 P.M. If there are special circumstances preventing you from starting work at 4 P.M., please let me know immediately. Otherwise, I expect that, going forward, you will report to work on time.

2. Four weeks ago you received a memo reminding you to arrive at work on time. Since then, you have been late 12

days and absent one day. This is your second and final reminder. You are to report to work by 4 P.M. every day for the next two weeks or you will be fired. Your continued employment after that date will depend upon your maintaining an outstanding on-time record.

IN SHORT

Bad news *can* be conveyed gracefully and effectively. Remember to respect your reader and to be sincere when your purpose is to correct, adjust, reject, refuse, remind, or demand.

Skill Building Until Next Time

Listen to how people refuse, reject, warn, and complain in their conversations. What techniques do speakers use to get the response they desire? After reading this chapter, can you tell what people do well and what they do poorly in these situations?

CHAPTER | 10

Employees are often
called upon to explain
how to do things, both
orally and in writing.
This chapter will show
you how to write clear
and effective procedures
and instructions.

WRITING PROCEDURES AND INSTRUCTIONS

*"The first step in writing instructions is figuring out
who your readers/users will be. You can't determine
what information you need to include or where to start
unless you know what your readers do and do not
know."*

John Brereton and Margaret Mansfield

Every new piece of equipment you buy
comes with a set of instructions. If those instructions aren't clear,
or if they're missing a step, you might have some serious difficulty using that equipment—and you or someone else may even end up
getting hurt.

Time, money, customers, your job, and the jobs of others—there's a
lot at stake in writing instructions. That's why it's critical to get it right,
absolutely right, before giving written instructions to others.

KNOW YOUR READERS

The first step in writing a set of instructions or explaining procedures
should be familiar to you by now: **identify your audience.** Who will be

reading these instructions or procedures? What do these readers need to know, and why? At what level of technicality or familiarity should you be writing for those readers?

Your instructions will be most successful if you consider your audience and determine the **"lowest common denominator"** of knowledge. If all readers know A, most know B, and only some know C, you can't write to the level of B or C—you *must* write to level A. If you don't, those readers who know A but don't know B or C will not be able to follow your directions.

Writing instructions is the one time that it's okay to risk wasting your readers' time by telling them things they may already know. Readers will simply skip over what's familiar. They can quickly separate new information from old. But what you can't do is omit what someone *may not* know.

BE THOROUGH

When writing instructions or procedures, you should be as thorough as possible. With your lowest common denominator in mind, list and explain *every* step of the process for someone *at that level.* For example, let's return to the instructions for a coffee machine.

> **Know Your Audience**
> Ask yourself, "What do my readers need to know, and why?" Find the lowest common denominator and write to that level.

Let's say you got a new machine in your employee lounge and you want to write directions for its use. Most readers, you might assume, have a coffee machine at home, but you can't be sure. Maybe one or two people don't. Maybe some people only drink tea and have never used a coffee machine. Thus, the lowest common denominator—the level at which you must write—is made up of people who have *never* used a coffee machine before. So the instructions will have to be very detailed if you want to be sure you will always have a decent cup of coffee. Your coworkers who've never used such a machine may not know what a coffee machine filter looks like, let alone how to insert it. So a step like "Insert filter" is not detailed enough to guide those users. Instead, you should write something like the following:

Pull out the brown filter basket, located directly above the coffee pot, and insert a single filter (filters are kept in the cabinet above the coffee machine). The filter should fit snugly in the basket.

It's much more detailed—and far more effective.

MAKE INSTRUCTIONS EASY TO FOLLOW

In addition to being written for the right audience, good instructions are also easy to follow. Four strategies will make your instructions easier to read and understand.

1. **"Signpost" your readers.** Guide your readers by offering signposts—indications that they're on (or off) the right track. For example, "Take Route 1 to Main Street" is not nearly as helpful as the paragraph below, which offers several signposts to help show readers the way:

   Take Route 1 five miles (approximately 10 minutes) to Main Street. Look for the YMCA on your left; Y Street is the next intersection after the YMCA. (If you pass the gas station, you have gone too far.)

2. **Use lists.** As you learned in Chapter 6, lists are easier to follow than straight narrative. Make each step a separate item on the list. Don't worry about having too many steps—the more, the better, because the more isolated each step is, the easier it is to perform— and the easier your instructions are to follow. Of course, it's also crucial to list the steps in **chronological order**. This is a must! Steps that are out of order in a list will confuse readers and may even endanger them.

3. **Use specific information.** Use exact names and numbers (times, distances, sizes, etc.) whenever possible. If you are vague, your readers may have trouble. For example, "Submit your evaluations to Human Resources" is not nearly as clear as "Submit your evaluations to Deana Brown in Human Resources, Room 112." The more specific your instructions, the more effectively people can carry them out.

4. **Use warnings.** Help your readers—and help keep them safe—by providing warnings or cautions when appropriate. For example,

you might include a warning like the following: "WARNING: If the valve is not in the 'off' position, pressure build-up may cause the pipe to burst." Make sure the wording of your warning is appropriate for the situation. For example, you might use the word "Caution" if the consequences are not serious; "Warning" if a serious problem or injury may result: and "Danger!" if serious physical injury or other harm is very likely to occur. Make sure your warnings stand out either through shading, color, or other graphic techniques.

THREE-PART STRUCTURE

Instructions should generally have three parts: an introduction, a body, and a conclusion.

Introduction

Good instructions have an introduction that provides important information for the user. At a minimum, your introduction should tell users what the instructions are for: "How to clear a paper jam" or "Procedure for clearing paper jams," for example. In this case, your introduction is really the same thing as your title.

If your instructions are more detailed, or if there's a particular reason people should follow these instructions, then an introduction should also tell readers *why the instructions are important*. For example, you might get a memo from payroll with the following introduction:

> Below are the procedures for completing and submitting time sheets. It is essential that you fill out the sheets properly. Errors on these sheets will mean errors on your paycheck. Be sure to fill out each sheet completely. Incomplete sheets will not be processed.

This introduction offers important information that will help readers follow the procedures more carefully.

Introductions for instructions may also:

- Indicate how long the procedure will take
- Describe what the finished product should be like
- Mention a particularly important item that might be overlooked or that needs to be emphasized ("Be sure to pay particular attention to the deadlines listed below")
- List any materials that the reader may need to follow the instructions—forms, tools, etc.

Body

The body of a piece of writing is where the bulk of information is found. The body of a set of instructions, then, lists the specific steps of the procedure *in chronological order.* The body can vary greatly in length depending upon how many steps there are in the process—and how detailed those steps are.

Conclusion

Good instructions will also provide a brief conclusion that tells readers:

- Whom to call if they have any trouble
- What to expect next or from the results
- How to follow up, if necessary, on the procedure (for example, "If you do not receive a reimbursement check within three weeks, contact Ms. Miller in accounting at extension 345.")

Sample Instructions

Here's a short set of instructions that includes an introduction, body, and conclusion. Notice the examples that make it easy to follow:

Requesting Time Off

All employees are entitled to vacation and personal days as described in the Employee Benefits Package. (If you do not have a package, please contact Brenda Greshock, Benefits Manager, at extension 332.) To request time off for personal or vacation days, please follow the procedures below.

1. Pick up a "Time Off Request" form from Human Resources (Room 11).
2. Fill out the form completely. Don't forget to sign it.
3. Get your supervisor's signature on the form.
4. Return the form to Annette Lowes in Human Resources.

IMPORTANT NOTE: Time Off Requests take approximately 3-5 days to process. Please submit your requests at least one week prior to the date(s) for which you are requesting time off.

You will receive a copy of your request, marked "Approved" or "Rejected," within one week of submission. If your request has been rejected, a detailed explanation of that rejection will be included.

If you have any questions, please contact Jude Raimes, Assistant Director of Human Resources, at extension 553.

BE COMPLETE

It is crucial to include *all* relevant information in your instructions. For example, take a look at the following set of instructions:

Procedures for Tuition Reimbursement
1. Fill out an application.
2. Get your supervisor's approval.
3. Submit the application to Human Resources.
4. When you receive your grade for the course, bring it to payroll along with a copy of your approved application.
5. Specify whether you want to be reimbursed by a separate check or have the amount added directly to your payroll check.

If you were to follow these procedures, you might not get your reimbursement. Why not? Because one vital piece of information is missing from this set of instructions: *when* the application should be submitted. If there's a deadline for submitting that application and you miss it, you won't get your money back. Also, these instructions don't tell you where to get the application form, if that form has a particular name or number, or where you should indicate how you want to be reimbursed. Is there a separate form to fill out or a box to check on the application?

Furthermore, the writer of these instructions assumes readers know what types of classes and employees qualify for tuition reimbursement. If there are limitations, readers need to know.

Practice A

On a separate sheet of paper, revise the tuition reimbursement instructions listed above so that they are more effective. Include a brief introduction and conclusion.

TEST YOUR INSTRUCTIONS

The best way to make sure your instructions are complete, thorough, and easy to follow is to test them. Before you hand over instructions to someone else, follow your instructions yourself. Don't do what you know how to do; do only what you've written, exactly how you've written it. Does it work? If not, revise. Then show your instructions to someone else, preferably someone who has never done the task you're explaining. Are your instructions clear? Easy to follow? Complete? See if your reader can perform that task without any trouble. If your reader has difficulty, revise your instructions again—and then find another reader to test them. Repeat this procedure until readers can follow your instructions with ease.

> **Test Time**
> When you've finished your instructions, give them a test run. Can someone follow them without difficulty?

PRACTICE B

Your company is expecting some people from out of town and you have been asked to write up instructions for how to get to your office. Write these instructions, assuming, for the sake of this exercise, that everyone is coming from your home. Remember, if it's possible that even *one* person has never made this trip before, you have to include *all* the steps and lots of details.

Possible Answers for Practice Exercises
Practice A

Procedures for Tuition Reimbursement:
All full-time employees are eligible for tuition reimbursement for undergraduate course work towards an AA, BA, or BS degree or graduate coursework that is work-related. To receive reimbursement for tuition expenses, **you must submit a completed Tuition Reimbursement Application Form to Human Resources *before* you register for class.** In addition, you must earn a C or better in the class in order to be eligible for reimbursement. Detailed instructions follow:

1. Get a Tuition Reimbursement Application Form from Debbie in Human Resources.
2. Fill out the form *completely.* Incomplete forms cannot be approved.
3. Have your supervisor sign the bottom of the form.
4. Make a copy of the completed form to keep for your records. You will need this form to pick up your reimbursement.
5. Submit the original completed application to Lorraine in Human Resources. Human Resources must have this form on file before you register for the course.
6. When you receive your grade report for the course, take it to Jennifer or Andrew in payroll along with a copy of your completed application.
7. Request a Reimbursement Receipt form from payroll. Indicate on this form whether you wish to be reimbursed by separate check or have the amount added directly to your payroll check. Give this form, your grade report, and your application form to Jennifer or Andrew for processing. (You should make a copy of all forms for your own records before submitting them to payroll.)

If you complete all of these steps you should receive your reimbursement check in the next payroll period. Please call Lorraine in Human Resources at extension 4488 if you have any questions about the procedure.

Practice B

Answers will vary, but a good set of instructions should be in some sort of list, should include specific names and numbers ("go through three stop lights and turn left onto Mulberry Road"), and should signpost readers ("the office is 1/4 mile past the large 'Drink Milk' billboard"). Your instructions should also pass a usability test. If you give them to someone else, that person should be able to get to your office from your home without difficulty.

IN SHORT

Good instructions are vital for good workplace communication. Make sure your instructions take readers step by step through the process and that each step is explained carefully and clearly. Know your audience, and be thorough in completing the introduction, body, and conclusion of your instructions. Signpost your readers and help them along by being specific and by numbering or bulleting each individual step.

Skill Building Until Next Time

Look through magazines to find "how-to" articles. Notice how these articles are written and identify their audience. (Note: If it's a specialized magazine, like *Gourmet*, notice that some terms, like "blanch," may not be explained because the audience is specialized and readers are expected to know specialized cooking terms.) What strategies do these articles use to make the instructions easy to follow? How do writers use introductions and conclusions to frame their instructions?

CHAPTER | 11

Reviews, particularly of employees, are often conducted in the workplace. This chapter will give you strategies for writing effective reviews at work.

REVIEWING

"Assertions are fine, but unless you support them with evidence, they remain simply assertions. So, assert, then support; assert, then support; assert, then support."

John Trimble

I f you're thinking of going to the theater, how do you decide which movie to see? Most people look for some kind of critical reaction or judgment. What did their friends think of it? What do the papers say about it? We often look to reviews (formal or informal) to help us decide on everything from what book to read to what car to buy.

Reviews also play an important role in the workplace. People, places, programs, and products all get reviewed, and because a review can help decide the fate of that person, place, program, or product, it's very important that it be written well.

Reviews, unlike reports, are marked by **personal opinion, impression, or reaction**. A report demands **objectivity**—writers should describe only what they have seen, heard, or learned. A review, on the other hand, demands **subjectivity**—writers should describe what they think or feel about something. A report says "Here's what happened." A review says "Here is what I think, and here's why." What distinguishes a good review from a bad one is the "why"—how much and what kind of evidence is offered to *support* the writer's assertions.

In general, a review should do the following:

- Make a strong, clear assertion about the person, place, or thing being reviewed
- Offer a brief explanation of why an issue is being reviewed, if applicable
- Offer strong evidence that supports the opening assertion

MAKING YOUR ASSERTION

When you are faced with the task of writing a review, you may want to begin by filling in the blank in a sentence that will help you take a clear position on the subject: "I think X," or "I feel X." Here's an example:

I think wearing hairnets is _____.
I feel wearing hairnets is _____.

The Difference Between Reports and Reviews

Reports are objective (based on fact).
Reviews are subjective (based on opinion).

Try to fill in the blank with as many different words and ideas as possible. Then, find the word or idea that sums up all of the words and ideas you've listed. (This will have to be a *general* word or idea so that it can serve as a topic sentence; see Chapter 3 if you need a refresher.)

SUPPORT YOUR ASSERTIONS

A strong review offers specific, detailed support for its assertions. For example, take a look at the following review of an entry-level employee:

Adrian has proven to be an excellent sorting machine operator.

One of Adrian's strengths is that he is a quick learner. Our former sorting machine operator took a week to train; Adrian was ready to begin after just two days even though he'd had no previous sorting machine experience. When Quincy Epstein had an emergency, Adrian volunteered to cover his shift and learned Epstein's routine in just a few minutes. And when I gave him the machine manual to review, he memorized all the troubleshooting procedures by the end of the week.

I'm also impressed by Adrian's desire to help others. When he hears that someone is having a problem, he immediately offers to help. Recently, when Jennifer was backlogged, he asked if I would mind if he spent an hour or two helping her catch up since he was a little bit ahead for the day.

Notice that this review begins with a clear assertion that shows how the writer feels about Adrian. This is also a good review because it offers specific, detailed support for its assertion.

There is one potential problem with this review, though: Because it is filled with nothing but praise for Adrian, it may make Adrian seem a little too good to be true.

INCLUDE BOTH GOOD AND BAD

A review that is entirely one-sided (either completely positive or completely negative) might not be taken as seriously as one that shows some balance. This doesn't mean that you can't write a good or bad review; it simply means you should show that you're discriminating—that *you've looked for the bad in the good or the good in the bad.*

It's rare, but certainly not impossible, that a person, place, or thing is completely negative, without one redeeming quality, or that someone or something is perfect, without a single flaw. Still, a good review not only points out what is good but also what could be better. If you write a rave review of Adrian and point out one area in which Adrian could improve, your review will generally have much more credibility—and be much more useful—than a review that finds no room for improvement. Your review will then show that:

- Adrian is not a robot (Adrian is human and has faults).
- You have the ability to distinguish between good and bad, between levels of service or performance.

In order to make the review of Adrian more credible, then, you might add a sentence like:

> I would like to see Adrian improve in one area: assertion. He is so eager to please us all that sometimes he lets others take advantage of him.

Notice how in pointing out a weakness in Adrian, you've also pointed out a strength. But you don't have to; you could say:

> One area where Adrian has to improve is in math. I have caught many errors in his calculations in weekly reports.

Whatever the case, you could then make suggestions to correct the problem:

> I would be happy to talk with Adrian about this if you think it would be appropriate.

> Perhaps the company would allow Adrian to take a math refresher course at the local community college.

PRACTICE

1. On a separate sheet of paper, write a brief review of the last movie you saw. Be sure to use strong specific support for your main idea.
2. Write a review of your supervisor. (He or she gets to review you, so now it's your turn!) Be sure to use strong, specific support for your main idea.

Possible Answers for Practice Exercises

1. Your review might be a positive or a negative one, but make sure it indicates from the beginning whether you give the movie thumbs up or thumbs down. It should also give your specific reasons for liking or not liking the movie. And generally, you should be able to find at least one good point in a bad movie, or one thing that was not up to par in a good one.

2. Your review will be different, of course, but here's an example:

> Ted is an ideal supervisor. He is patient and fair. When there was a disagreement between two assemblers, for example, he listened carefully to both sides and helped them work out a compromise. He lets us know exactly what he expects from us and then if we don't come through, he always gives us a second chance. He also shows respect for us. He never criticizes us or our work in front of others and always asks for our opinions. Finally, he's a great supervisor because he understands when family obligations and emergencies interfere with work. Last month, for example, when my daughter became ill at school, he personally covered my shift so I could leave early. The only thing I would change about Ted is that he is sometimes forgetful. Last week, for example, he forgot to tell us about the change in the meeting time for the union meeting. Still, he's a terrific boss and I am very glad to be working for him.

IN SHORT

Reviewing is an important function of writing for work. A good review makes a strong, clear assertion about what the writer thinks or feels and is supported by strong, specific evidence. It avoids being completely one-sided and may offer recommendations.

Skill Building Until Next Time

Read some reviews in a national newspaper or magazine: restaurant, movie, performance, book, or car reviews. Look carefully at how the experts do it.

CHAPTER | 12

Much of what people
write for work is meant
to convince others to
think or act in a certain
way. The strategies you
learn in this chapter
will help you write
persuasively.

CONVINCING

"The first step in persuasion is getting someone to listen."

Peter Elbow and Pat Belanoff

So much of what people write for work requires them to convince others to take action or approve of an idea. Whether it's "selling" a product or an idea, or proposing a project or a pay raise, convincing is an essential workplace writing function. The better you are at it, the more effective you will be at getting what you want.

This chapter will focus on how you can convince others in the following types of situations:

- You could really use some new equipment in your work area. How do you convince your supervisor to purchase what you need?

- You'd like to be transferred to another team or department. How do you convince your supervisor to approve the move?
- The charity you support is holding a benefit. How do you convince coworkers to participate?

BEGIN BY PREWRITING

Clear answers to your prewriting questions are essential if you are to write something that's convincing. The ability to persuade others is rooted in a clear understanding of your audience and purpose. Exactly whom are you trying to convince? The more specific you can be about your audience, the better you will be able to determine the wants and needs of your readers. And the more you know what your readers want and need, the easier it is to show how what *you* want fills *their* desires or needs.

Once you've pinpointed your audience, brainstorm about your purpose. Clearly, your main goal is to convince. But what exactly do you want to convince your readers to think or do? Here is an expanded list of verbs to help you clarify your purpose:

Purpose—to convince someone to:

help	call	register
send	visit	change
buy	agree	implement
do	write	permit
choose	approve	start
allow	pay	end

Many other verbs might apply, but this list should help you get started. Once your audience and purpose are clear, use these four strategies to convince your readers:

- show benefits
- provide specific evidence
- anticipate objections
- request a clear and specific action

SHOW BENEFITS

Once your audience and purpose are clear, the next step is to clarify exactly how your readers will benefit from doing what you ask. True, people will often do things for you just because they want to make you happy. But at work, people generally need to know that there are clear work-related benefits before they will agree to do what you ask. You know how you'll benefit from what you want; now, how will the reader or the company benefit? Brainstorm a list of as many benefits as possible, even though you might not use them all.

For example, if you want new equipment—a new industrial floor polisher, for example—you might list the following benefits:

- It will save time.
- It will save money now.
- It will save money in the future.

These are three clear benefits for the company and good reasons for management to agree to your request.

PROVIDE SPECIFIC EVIDENCE

So you've told your readers that they will get certain benefits from agreeing to do what you ask. Why should they believe you? How do they know, for example, that a new polisher will save time and money? The answer, of course, is to provide specific evidence for your claims. To support the claims about the polisher, you might add the following information:

- New industrial polishers cover twice as much floor space as our current polisher, so they polish twice as much floor in the same amount of time.
- New industrial polishers are more powerful, so they give a stronger shine in less time.
- We would be able to stop spending money on replacement parts and repairs for our current polisher, which cost us $800 last month alone.
- New industrial polishers come with extended service warrantees, so repair costs in the future will be minimal.

Remember, your evidence can come in many forms—details, statistics, examples, results, definitions, comparisons, quotations, etc. Support your assertions with strong, compelling evidence.

ANTICIPATE OBJECTIONS

If what you want requires people to give up time, energy, or money—*especially* if you want them to spend money—they are probably going to have reservations or objections to what you want them to do. And if they are going to have to get approval from someone else, *that* person might have reservations and objections as well. You're much more likely to convince people if you acknowledge and overcome their reservations and objections right from the beginning.

For example, if you want to convince your supervisor that your company needs a training manual in Spanish, chances are that even if your supervisor agrees that it's a good idea, she will have reservations about spending the time and money to have someone translate the manual. You might address those objections by saying something like the following:

> Of course, it will require time and money to translate the manual. But over half of our employees are native speakers of Spanish, and many have only elementary reading skills in English. I have spent more hours in the last few months explaining things that are clearly written in our manual than a person would spend translating the manual.

Notice how this paragraph acknowledges the reader's reservation and then overcomes it by showing how it's really not an issue; in fact, translating the manual would *save* time and money for the company. Addressing objections in this way is an essential component of any piece of writing that aims to convince.

REQUEST A CLEAR AND SPECIFIC ACTION FROM YOUR READER

Another key element of persuasive writing is to request a specific action from your readers. You've asked for what you want; you've shown readers exactly how they will benefit; now, as you conclude, *tell readers exactly what you want them to do.* For example, you might write:

> Please approve a purchase order for a new industrial floor polisher. A page from our supplier's catalog is attached.

Or:

> A Spanish version of our training manual would be very helpful to me and to the entire staff. Please approve this project.

Don't assume readers will figure out exactly what you want; tell them as clearly as possible what action you'd like them to take. The more direct and clear you are about it, the more likely you are to get people to do what you want them to do. (Of course, be reasonable. You can't say "Please hire me immediately and give me a $200,000 signing bonus." But you can say "Please let me know when I may come in for an interview. I look forward to working with you.")

CATCH YOUR READERS' ATTENTION

If your relationship to your readers is not a very formal one, or if the matter that you write about is not extremely serious or formal, try an introduction that catches the readers' attention. You might highlight the greatest benefit of what you are proposing, mention something readers would like to see happen, make a comparison, or ask a question that appeals to your readers' emotions. For example, let's take another look at the extraordinary request from Chapter 8:

> Time is money—and your time could mean money that's desperately needed for important medical research and services. I'm writing to ask for your time. As you may know, I volunteer at the Children's Hospital. Next month, the hospital is sponsoring a 5K run/walk. Will you participate? We need runners and walkers as well as volunteers to cover registration and t-shirt distribution. The run/walk is on Sunday, May 10, and starts at 9 a.m. If you'd like to participate, please call me at extension 3035. The registration deadline for participation is April 20. Please help us help children.

Notice that this memo doesn't appeal to the reader's desire to do a good job or improve business. Instead, the memo appeals to the reader's desire to help others, to participate in a good cause (an indirect personal benefit). Notice also how this memo starts off with a play on the well known sentence "Time is money." This is a rather unusual approach, especially in comparison to some of the standard topic sentences you've seen in this book. But it's appropriate and effective for this kind of informal memo. (You'll learn more about this type of introduction in Chapter 17.) The bottom line is, catchy introductions will grab your readers' attention and get them to read your communication. And if you've aroused a powerful emotion, readers are more likely to be convinced to do what you ask.

PRACTICE

1. There's an internal promotion and you want the job. On a separate sheet of paper, write a letter to the department manager convincing her to consider you for the position.
2. You want union members to vote a certain way on an important issue. Write them a memo that convinces them to do what you want. (If you don't belong to a union, create a similar situation that applies to your work.)

Possible Answers to Practice Exercises

1. Dear Mrs. Williams:

I would like to be considered for the position of forklift crew foreman. I have been a forklift operator for 15 years and have seen everything that could possibly go wrong on the factory grounds. I have trained many new forklift drivers and for several years I led a small forklift crew for another company. I realize I have only been an employee of Forklift United for 6 months, but I assure you I am thoroughly familiar with all the policies and procedures here, and I have already established an excellent relationship with my coworkers. With my years of experience and my dedication to the job, I would be a very effective foreman. Please let me know when I should come by for an interview.

2. Answers will vary. Your answer is a good one if you:

- show a clear purpose
- discuss the benefits to your readers
- anticipate their objections
- provide specific evidence to support your main idea

IN SHORT

Convincing requires you to show your readers exactly how they will benefit from doing what you want them to do. You need to provide evidence for your assertions, and you also have to address and overcome reservations and objections. Conclude by requesting clear, specific, and appropriate action from your readers.

Skill Building Until Next Time

Much of the mail you receive attempts to convince you—to buy a product, support a charity, renew a subscription. Look at how these letters try to convince. What benefits do they show you? How do they address and overcome your reservations and objections? What action would they like you to take?

SECTION 3

WORKPLACE WRITING FORMATS

Now that you know how to convey your main idea clearly and concisely and how to get across various kinds of messages, it's time to work on the *structure* of your message. Most of what you write for work will be presented in one of these basic formats:

- Letters
- Memos
- Reports
- Proposals
- Electronic mail
- Websites

Each of these formats has its own rules for presentation. The chapters in this section will show you these rules and how to make the most of them.

CHAPTER | 13

Letters are used to communicate with others outside your company and for official correspondence within your company. This chapter will show you the parts of business letters and their most common formats.

LETTERS

"A letter shows the man it is written to as well as the man it is written by."

Lord Chesterfield

Often what people say in a workplace letter is something that could have been said in person or on the phone. But if it's something important—something that they'll want to refer to or reference later; something that involves money, contracts or obligations; or something that they'll want to have proof of having said or done—it must be put in writing. That's why most correspondence with others outside the company is in the form of a standard business letter.

Chapters 7–12 discussed the various functions a letter or other communication may have—requesting, reminding, reviewing, convincing, and so on. This chapter shows you the specific formats those letters may have.

Letters follow a certain format for two reasons:

- To provide readers with certain necessary information: who wrote to whom, when, and regarding what topic
- To help organize information neatly

In addition, because business letters have followed a certain format for so long, readers expect to find certain information in certain places. Following the established format makes your letters reader-friendly.

A WORD ABOUT NEATNESS

For better or worse, in letters written at work, *how you present what you say* often matters as much as *what you say*. A reader who receives a sloppy letter with typographical errors, stray pen marks, and text that runs off the bottom of the page may be tempted to throw the letter out without even reading it. In business, first impressions count—especially in writing.

Neatness Counts

Make a good first impression by ensuring that your letter has no typos, that it is centered properly on the page, and that the paragraphs do not look crowded.

This means that when you're writing for work, *neatness* counts—and it counts for quite a lot. Readers will form an opinion of you and your company simply from the appearance of your letter, and this can make all the difference in how seriously your readers treat what you have to say.

If a letter of recommendation is sloppy, for example, it will undermine that recommendation. That's not fair to the person who's being reviewed in the letter. It also says a lot about the writer of the letter. Sloppy typing and presentation sends the message that you don't pay attention to detail, that you don't care about appearances, and that you don't respect your reader enough to be neat. So, here are a few general rules about presentation:

1. *Proofread* any letter before you send it out. And proofread it not just once, but twice—even three times. Get someone else to look it over for you as well.

2. Try to *center your letter on the page* to avoid having a large block of empty white space at the top or bottom.

3. *Avoid excessive margins* and *don't crowd your writing* to the edges of the page. In general, margins should be 1½ inches all around.

PARTS OF A BUSINESS LETTER

Business letters can have up to 11 parts. You may not use all of them every time, but you should use most of them most of the time:

- Writer's address
- Date
- Inside address
- *Re:* or Subject
- Salutation
- Body
- Close
- Signature
- Steno line/File number
- Enclosure
- CC/Distribution

The parts are described below in the order in which they should appear in a letter.

Writer's Address

If your letter will not be sent on company letterhead, make sure your company's name and address is the first item on your letter. This section should include two items:

- your company name
- your company address

This way your reader knows immediately who has sent the letter. Write out all the words in this address (write *Street*, not *St.*) except the abbreviations for Mr., Mrs., Ms., Dr., and the state (*IN* instead of *Indiana*). Here's an example:

Regal Manufacturing
222 Chestnut Lane
Cooperstown, OH 01101

Date

Next, type the month, day, and year of the letter. Write out the full name of the month (*September*, not *Sept.* or *9*) and use the number for the day (*12*, not *twelfth* or *12th*). Don't include the day of the week.

Correct	Incorrect
April 3, 2000	Tues. 4/3/00
	April third, 2000
	April 3rd, '00

Inside Address

Write the full name, title, company, and address of the reader. Don't abbreviate except for Mr., Ms., Mrs., and Dr. and the name of the state. You may choose to omit Mr., Ms., or Mrs., but Dr. should remain. (If you are unsure whether to use Mrs. or Ms. and can't find out via a phone call, use Ms.)

Ms. Emily Warren
Manager
LMN Cleaners
557 Summit Avenue
Whitehall, NY 10099

Re: or Subject

Re: is an abbreviation for *regarding*. The *re:* line (often called the *subject line*) is a quick reference telling the reader what the letter is about. The *re:* line is not mandatory, but it's very helpful and it's almost always used in correspondence regarding legal matters or past due accounts. The *re:* line should be no more than a few words and is usually underlined. It can range from an account number to several words describing the letter's main subject:

Re: Account # 4366

Re: Revised Safety Standards

Salutation

The salutation is the greeting or opening of the letter. Begin with the word "Dear" and be sure your salutation properly reflects the formality of your relationship to the reader. Follow the salutation with a colon (:). Here are some guidelines for determining the proper salutation:

If:	Use:	Example:
You are not on a first-name basis with the reader	Mr./Ms./Mrs. and the reader's last name	*Dear Mr. Jones*
You don't know the reader's name	Sir/Madam, or use the person's title	*Dear Sir/Madam* or *Dear Customer Service Representative*
You know the reader's name but don't know whether the reader is male or female, do not assume or guess.	Mr./Ms. ___	*Dear Mr./Ms. Jones*

Body

The body of the letter (your actual message) is usually single spaced, with double spacing between paragraphs.

Close

This is your "goodbye." There are several options for how to close your letter, and again, your close should reflect the formality of your relationship with your reader. The following list of closing words and phrases is ranked in order of formality, with number 1 being the most formal:

1. Very truly yours,
2. Yours truly,
3. Sincerely yours,
4. Sincerely,
5. Cordially,
6. Best regards/Best wishes,

7. Regards,

8. Best,

9. Yours,

Number 4, "Sincerely," is the most common close used in everyday business communications.

Only the first word of a close gets capitalized, and be sure to put a comma after the close.

Correct	Incorrect
Very truly yours,	Very Truly Yours
Best regards,	Best Regards,

Signature

Four lines beneath your close, type your full name and, directly beneath that, your title. Sign your full name in the space between the two. However, if you are on a first-name basis with the reader, just your first name will do for your signature. Do make sure you sign your letter. Letters without signatures are generally not considered valid, and if someone else signs for you, it shows that you don't consider the reader (or your letter) important enough to sign it yourself.

Steno Line/File Number

If someone else types your letter for you—or if you are typing a letter for someone else—this should be indicated on your letter. One or two lines beneath your signature, the typist should write the initials of the letter sender in capitals followed by a slash (/) and then his or her own initials in lower case letters. Thus if your initials are JTE, and a typist with the initials DF typed your letter for you, the steno line would look like this:

JTE/df

If you type your own correspondence, there's absolutely no need for a steno line.

Sometimes, in combination with or in place of the steno line, there is a file name or number to indicate how the document has been saved, filed, or stored on the computer (for example, C:/A&D/Letters/invoice). Both conventions (the steno line and the file name or number) are used primarily to help track down documents and document errors.

Enclosure

If you're enclosing documents with your letter, you need to include an enclosure line. A few lines below your signature or steno line, type "Enclosure" or "Enc." against the left-hand margin. Then, list the documents that are enclosed. Here's an example:

Enclosures: Safety Guidelines
                     Employee Handbook

The enclosure line is used to clearly indicate what items have been sent along with the letter. This way, readers can be sure they've received everything they're supposed to with your letter. If you don't enclose anything else with the letter, then you don't need to type an enclosure line.

CC/Distribution

If people other than the addressee are to receive copies of your letter, and you want your reader to know that these people are receiving copies, then use the "CC" line. "CC" stands for "carbon copy," a leftover from the days before copy machines when duplicates were made with carbon copy sheets. For example, if you were to write to someone and wanted to send a copy of that letter to your boss, you would double space down from the enclosure line (or whatever is the last line of your letter) and type the name of your boss:

CC: Jan Gallagher

If you want to copy several people, there are two choices for how to list those names: You can list these people in alphabetical order, or you can list them according to rank. You can also show their titles. In fact, if the addressee is not likely to know who these people are (or if those people being cc'd and the addressee are not likely to know each other), you should show their titles, as in the following example:

cc: Erik Lucas, President, AMD Financing
     Jennifer Alexander, Manager, Mortgages Plus

Here, the cc's are ranked by title, not by alphabet. Generally, people who are mentioned in your letter or people who should know about the information in your letter should be copied. (Note: "CC" can be printed in capital or lower case letters.)

COMMON BUSINESS LETTER FORMATS

These 11 parts of business letters are usually laid out on the page in one of two ways: block format or semi-block format.

Block Format

With the block format, each of the letter's 11 parts (including every paragraph in the body of the letter) is set against the left-hand margin. This is the simplest format.

Semi-Block Format

The semi-block format places most of the parts at the left-hand margin, but not all. The writer's address, date, *re:* line, close, and signature start at a tab in the middle of the page (usually the 4-inch mark). Paragraphs in the body of the letter can be typed at the left-hand margin or they can be indented five spaces (this is often called the *modified* semi-block format).

On the next pages you will see the same letter printed in both block format and modified semi-block format.

Block Letter

Kisha Miller
Kruger Corporation
203 Elm Street
Smithtown, PA 19000

March 30, 2000

Customer Service Department
Ermine Parts Company
325 Baker Boulevard
Johnstown, PA 19009

Re: <u>Shipping error</u>

Dear Sir/Madam:

We recently ordered several replacement parts for our model 224 sorting machine. The shipment we received today had the right parts but for the wrong model. We are returning those parts to you by overnight mail. In the meantime, we have enclosed a copy of our original order and a copy of the packaging slip for the order we actually received.

We need these parts as soon as possible and would appreciate a prompt shipment of the correct parts.

Thank you.

Sincerely,

Kisha Miller

Enc: Copy of order
     Copy of packaging slip

CC: Charles Down, Facilities Manager

Modified Semi-Block Letter

Kisha Miller
Kruger Corporation
203 Elm Street
Smithtown, PA 19000

March 30, 2000

Customer Service Department
Ermine Parts Company
325 Baker Boulevard
Johnstown, PA 19009

Re: <u>Shipping error</u>

Dear Sir/Madam:

We recently ordered several replacement parts for our model 224 sorting machine. The shipment we received today had the right parts but for the wrong model. We are returning those parts to you by overnight mail. In the meantime, we have enclosed a copy of our original order and a copy of the packaging slip for the order we actually received.

We need these parts as soon as possible and would appreciate a prompt shipment of the correct parts.

Thank you.

Sincerely,

Kisha Miller

Enc: Copy of order
     Copy of packaging slip

cc: Charles Down, Facilities Manager

Letters of Two or More Pages

If your letter is more than one full page, the top of each additional page should include:

- The addressee's name
- The page number
- The date

This can be typed across the top of the page (all on one line) or on the first three lines of the page, at the left-hand margin, right-hand margin, or (if all on one line) centered. Here are two examples:

John Francis, Nov. 21, 2000, page 2.   John Francis
                                        November 21, 2000
                                        Page 2

Company Style

Many companies choose a certain style for their letters. Find out if your company prefers block or semi-block or has some other format for letters. The more consistent a company is in how it presents itself to others, the greater the impression that the company cares about details and how it appears to the public.

PRACTICE

Take two letters from Chapters 7–12 and write or type them out in letter format. Make up the addresses. Use block format for one and semi-block or modified semi-block for the other. Be sure to choose something that could be sent as a *letter* rather than a memo.

Possible Answers for Practice Exercises

The next page shows a sample letter in block format.

Robert Smith
ABC Corporation
123 Elm Street
Smithtown, PA 19000

March 30, 2000

Kisha Miller
Kruger Corporation
203 Elm Street
Smithtown, PA 19000

Dear Ms. Miller:

Thank you for requesting information about the workbench stools. We are proud of our wide selection and affordable pricing. Our most recent catalog is enclosed. Should you wish to order from us, you can expect to receive shipment within 2–4 weeks for most models. Please let me know if you have any other questions or if I can be of further assistance. I look forward to your order.

Thank you.

Sincerely,

Robert Smith
Customer Service Representative

Enc: Catalog

IN SHORT

Letters that you write for work should have the standard business letter parts and, unless your company has its own standard practices, they should fit into one of the standard business letter formats: block, semi-block, or modified semi-block format. Remember that neatness counts, so proofread carefully.

Skill Building Until Next Time

Look at the letters you receive at home from various businesses. Do they have all of the standard letter parts? In the right order? Do they use block, semi-block, or modified semi-block formats? You should notice very little deviation from these formats.

CHAPTER | 14

Memos are used for most internal workplace communications. This chapter will show you the different parts of a memo and strategies for an easy-to-follow format.

MEMOS

"When you receive a letter or memo, one of the first things you probably respond to is its tone. Unlike technical reports, proposals, or manuals, this type of correspondence carries with it a personal voice."

Kristin Woolever

External communications usually take the form of letters; internal communications, on the other hand, usually take the form of memos. A memo is a "letter" that is sent internally, within companies or organizations.

You may also have the occasion to write an external memo—a memo to someone outside of your company. It might be a company that you regularly communicate with for reasons outside of your normal money-making business. For example, if you and two other companies share a security service for your building, communications regarding this security service would probably be sent in a memo instead of a letter.

The main difference between memos and letters is that memos are less formal. They shouldn't be used for official correspondence, such as a contract renewal; this kind of communication should take the form of a letter.

Like letters, memos can have a variety of subjects, purposes, and formats, and like letters, all memos have a certain number of required parts. But because memos are less formal, they have less than half as many parts as a letter.

These six parts fall into two main sections: the **heading** and the **body.** The heading shows who is writing to whom, when, and about what; the body then conveys the message.

THE HEADING

The heading of a memo should include the five parts listed below, in exactly this order:

- To
- From
- Date
- *Re:* or Subject line
- CC

To

List the names of everyone who will receive the memo. Include first *and* last names *and* titles (or departments) of recipients for formal memos or memos to superiors. (If you are writing an external memo, then you should include the name of the company that each recipient works for as well.) Even if the subject is not formal, include titles if you're not sure everyone on the list knows everyone else on the list. If all recipients know each other's names and positions, then you can use just the first initial and last name of each recipient. Here are some examples:

To: Ann Reed, President
Alex Alvarez, Manager

To: A. Reed
    A. Alvarez

To: Ann Reed, President, Widgets, Inc.
    Alex Alvarez, Manager, Supplies R Us

When you have several recipients, you have to decide how to list them. As with cc's on letters, you have two choices: list them alphabetically or by rank. Either order is acceptable.

If your memo is going to a lot of people, you don't have to list dozens of names. Instead, you can name the group or groups that the recipients belong to (so long as everyone in that group is getting the memo). Here are some examples:

To: All Employees

To: Production Managers
    Production Line Assistants

From

List the author(s) of the memo. You should generally list the name(s) and/or title(s) of the author(s) in the same way you've listed the name(s) and/or title(s) of the recipients. If the memo is from several people, follow the same rule: List them alphabetically or by rank. Again, list them in the same way you listed your recipients. There is no signature line in a memo, but authors still "sign" their memos before sending them out by writing their initials next to the "from" line. Here's an example:

From: Ellen Miggino **EM**

Date

List the month, date, and year just as you would in a letter (*March 28, 2000*, not *3/28/00* or *Mar. 28th '00*).

Re: or Subject

The *re:* or subject line is much the same as the *re:* line in a letter, with one important exception: In a memo, the *re:* line should be more specific. It should still be short enough to fit on one line, but it should give readers a better idea of the subject matter of the memo. For example, compare the two *re:* lines below:

RE: Workman's Compensation

RE: Changes in Workman's Compensation Benefits for
       maintenance personnel

The first *re:* line is fine for a letter but too vague for a memo. The second *re:* line, however, tells readers a lot more and therefore is better for a memo. Someone in maintenance, for example, may get dozens of memos a week regarding repairs. If all the *re:* lines simply said "Repairs," he or she wouldn't be able to distinguish at a glance which memos were new request for repairs, repeat requests for repairs, reports about repairs, etc. Specific *re:* lines help personnel instantly prioritize their internal mail. Besides, these are your coworkers, so you should want to be as reader-friendly as possible. A specific *re:* line gives them the specific subject of your communication without forcing them to read your first few sentences.

Distribution/CC

The distribution/CC part of a memo is just like the CC section of a letter. List those readers who are not direct recipients of your message but who should have a copy for their information or reference. The same rules apply for the order and format in which you list these names and/or titles.

THE BODY

The body of a memo is usually separated from the heading by a solid or dotted line or by several spaces. Some writers use a line of asterisks (*) or other symbols. Check with your company to see if there's a routine way of separating the heading from the body.

The body of a memo, like the body of a letter, is usually single spaced with double spacing between paragraphs. It also typically follows a four-part organizational pattern.

Organization

The body of a memo is generally broken up into four parts:

1. **Introduction.** State the general problem or issue. What is the memo about? What do you need to say *about* that subject? Make sure your main idea is clear.
2. **Statement of facts.** State the facts or discuss the problem or issue. Provide detailed support for the main idea.
3. **Argument.** Explain the importance or relevance of those facts. Why do they matter? What's at stake?
4. **Conclusion.** If your memo is on the longer side, summarize the main idea. Then, suggest or request an action. What should readers do? What action do you recommend be taken? In some cases, you will simply want to offer a name and number to call if readers have questions or need more information. In other cases, you may simply conclude with a thank you or other appropriate closing.

Unlike letters, which are rarely more than two pages long, memos are often considerably longer, sometimes running even as long as 20 pages. Memos also tend to be more informative while letters tend to be more persuasive. As a result, memos are often loaded with information. Be sure to employ readability strategies throughout the body of your memo. Organize your information into small, manageable chunks of information; provide headings; and use lists, tables, and graphs when possible.

Letters	Memos
Are typically written to people outside of the company	Are typically written to people within the company
Are usually short—less than two pages long	Vary in length from one paragraph to as many as 20 pages
Are often formal	Are often informal
Are usually more persuasive than informative	Are usually more informative than persuasive
Are signed by the sender	Are initialed by the sender
Are printed on official company letterhead	Are printed on standard white paper

Below are two memos that use this four-part organizational pattern and readability strategies. The first is a short memo you've seen before. Now that you're aware of this memo structure, re-read the memo and notice how it successfully includes each of these four parts. The second memo is considerably longer, but it, too, includes each of the four parts and uses readability strategies to make the memo reader friendly.

Notice how both memos offer a brief introduction, state the facts, discuss their relevance, and conclude with a call to action (the first memo) and a summary/thank you (the second memo).

MEMO

TO:	All Second- and Third-Shift Personnel
FROM:	Karen Hunt, Third-Shift Coordinator
DATE:	August 3, 2000
RE:	Run/Walk for Children's Hospital

Time is money—and your time could mean money that's desperately needed for important medical research and services. I'm writing to ask for your time. As you may know, I volunteer at the Children's Hospital. Next month, the hospital is sponsoring a 5K run/walk. Will you participate? We need runners and walkers as well as volunteers to cover registration and T-shirt distribution. The run/walk will be held on Sunday, September 17, and starts at 9:00 a.m. If you'd like to help, please call me at extension 3035. The registration deadline is April 20. Please help us help children in our community. Thanks.

MEMO • MEMO • MEMO • MEMO • MEMO • MEMO • MEMO

TO: Otis Jackson, President
         Claude Gavin, Director, Special Events
FROM: Annette Platier, Events Coordinator
DATE: September 19, 2000
RE: 5K Run/Walk Results
CC: Volunteer Coordinators

Sunday's third annual Children's Hospital 5K Run/Walk was our most successful fundraiser to date. We raised a record $840,389 and generated a great deal of publicity for the hospital.

Increased Participation

More than 25 local businesses sponsored approximately 420 participants, while more than 800 individuals ran or walked in this year's 5K event. This is more than twice the number of participants from last year and more than triple the number of participants from 1998. (See the table below for statistics for the past three years.) Our radio promotions, community bulletin board postings, and direct call campaigns—three new strategies employed this year—helped us reach a much larger audience and are responsible for this dramatic increase in participation.

Year	Corporations Participating	Participants from those Corporations	Individuals Participating	Total Participants	Funds Raised
1998	5	115	318	433	$235,984
1999	14	189	401	590	$552,921
2000	26	421	816	1236	$840,389

Pledge Matching

This year, for the first time, we asked participating companies to match pledges for all employees who participated. This program was also a tremendous success. Matching funds represented more than 25% of all monies raised. We owe a special thanks to our two "mega-sponsors," Digital Dynamics and

Greater Health Options, who together donated more than $60,000 in matching funds.

New Sponsors

In addition to the corporate matching program, this year we were able to recruit three important new sponsors who provided us with over $12,000 of services and supplies. Our three corporate sponsors included:

- D-Zine T-Shirts, who donated T-shirts for participants and volunteers.
- Superior Food and Beverage Services, who donated food and beverages for our runners and volunteers.
- Promotional Ventures Inc., who donated design and production services for our advertising campaign.

All three companies have agreed to donate their services and supplies again next year.

Thank you to everyone who helped make this event such an overwhelming success!

Level of Formality

As you learned earlier in this chapter, one of the main differences between memos and letters is their **level of formality.** The degree of formality of a document is determined by three key factors:

1. Word choice
2. Point of view
3. Format/design

Word Choice

Word choice is exactly that: the words the writer chooses to convey his or her ideas. For example, read the following sentences:

a. This is a risky situation.
b. This is a dangerous situation.
c. This is a perilous situation.

How are these three sentences different? All three of them show that the situation is uncertain and potentially harmful. But notice the differences in the words the writers chose to describe the situation. One describes the situation as *risky*, another as *dangerous*, and another as *perilous*.

Though each sentence conveys essentially the same idea, the **connotation** of each word makes for three rather different sentences. Connotation is a word's *implied* or *suggested* meaning. It refers to the social or emotional impact that the word carries. *Perilous* carries a much more serious connotation than *risky*; thus, you can conclude that the writer of sentence (c) is much more concerned about the situation than writer (a), while writer (b) is somewhere in between.

In workplace writing, the words you choose will convey your **tone** (your attitude towards the subject and audience) and your relationship to your reader. For example, look at the two sentences below:

a.   We need to get together to hammer out a new schedule.
b.   We need to meet to arrange a new schedule.

Notice that sentence (a) uses the words *get together* and *hammer out* while sentence (b) uses the words *meet* and *arrange*. Because sentence (b) uses more formal words, you can infer (conclude) that the writer of sentence (b) has a more formal relationship with the reader. You can also infer that putting together the schedule is a more formal or serious procedure in sentence (b) than it is in sentence (a).

In workplace writing, occasions for slang, or very informal language, are rare; occasions for very formal language and jargon (specialized or technical vocabulary) are much more common. Word choice in memos, however, should typically fall somewhere in the middle of the spectrum.

Point of View

Because memos are generally written from one coworker to another, there is a level of familiarity that should come across in your writing. In a memo, use the first person point of view to refer to yourself and the second person point of view to refer to your readers (see the chart below to review points of view). Your memo should clearly be *from* a person *to* a person.

Point of View	Pronouns	Effects
First Person	I, me, mine, we, our, us	Creates intimacy between reader and writer. Suggests subjectivity; based on the experience of the writer.
Second Person	You	Puts the reader in the writer's shoes.
Third Person	He, him, his; she, her, hers; it, its; they, them, theirs	Creates distance between the reader and writer. Suggests objectivity; not influenced by the thoughts and feelings of the writer.

Format/Design

The format of a memo also reinforces its degree of formality. The writer initials the memo rather than signing it, suggesting that the document is important but not "official." Memo styles are also less rigid; often, companies don't have a standard format for memos. Letters, on the other hand, must be written on official company letterhead. If you design your own memo format, aim for a style that is simple and uncluttered. Avoid playful fonts such as **Sand** or PEIGNOT. Instead, stick with standard, easy-to-read fonts such as Times New Roman or Arial. The format and design of your memo should reflect the appropriate level of formality.

PRACTICE

Rewrite two exercises from Chapters 7–12 as a memo. Be sure to use the proper format and an appropriate tone.

Possible Answer for Practice Exercise

MEMORANDUM

TO: Sharon Small, Assembler
FROM: Karen Hunt, Payroll Supervisor KH
DATE: July 29, 2000
RE: Recent errors in your paychecks
CC: Charles Good, Payroll Administrator

****

We deeply regret the recent error in your paychecks. We have discovered an error in your account on the payroll system and we have corrected the problem. Your future checks should include the overtime pay you are due. We have also prepared a check for the overtime pay that is owed to you. You may pick up that check tomorrow morning. Please stop by my office at your earliest convenience. (My office is located next to the Coke machine on the fourth floor.) I look forward to meeting you.

In Short

Memos are internal workplace communications that consist of a heading and body. The body of a memo has a four-part structure and often uses headings, lists, and tables or graphs to make its information more readable. They're less formal than letters and should use an appropriate personal tone.

Skill Building Until Next Time

Look carefully at the next memos you receive at work. Notice how the headings are arranged and how the information in the body is organized. Do the memos use any readability strategies? What kind of tone do they use? How else is the level of formality distinguished from a letter?

CHAPTER | 15

Reports are an important part of workplace writing and something you may need to write often. This chapter will show you the parts of a report and how these parts are formatted.

REPORTS

"Think of your intended readers as the real people they will be when they take your letter or report out of the 'in-box.' Only then can you decide intelligently what information and ideas to emphasize and in what order to present them."

Kevin J. Harty

Company executives can't be everywhere at once, yet they need to know what's happening in every department in order to keep business running smoothly. They could never do this without reports.

As an employee you may be responsible for reporting to management on a number of issues: progress on projects, production, incidents, accidents, and so on. Here's a short list of some of the types of reports you may have to write:

- Meeting reports (minutes)
- Progress reports

- Periodic reports
- Trip reports
- Production reports
- Incident reports
- Accident reports
- Work reports

Some of these reports are written on a regular basis (every day, week, month, or year). Many of these reports will come to you pre-formatted: you will simply have to fill in the appropriate information on the form. In other cases, you'll have to start from scratch. Either way, you should know the general format for reports and some specific report formats.

THE PURPOSE OF A REPORT

Reports are generally designed to tell readers:

1. What you saw or heard
2. What you did
3. What you learned

Your readers will then make a decision or take action based on your report.

REPORT FORMAT

Unlike letters or memos, most common workplace reports don't consist of numerous parts. They usually begin with three important pieces of information:

1. A short, simple title that indicates their subject, like "Work Report" or "Accident Report"
2. The author's name(s)
3. The date

Then, the rest of the report usually follows a three-part structure: introduction, body, and conclusion/recommendations.

Introduction

First, the beginning of a report introduces the subject and purpose of the report, often using a clear topic sentence like the following:

> This is a report of work-related accidents from January 1, 2000, through June 30, 2000.

Reports may also begin with a sentence that summarizes the information to be contained in the report:

> The number and type of work-related accidents for 1999 reflects an improvement in safety measures and standards.

If a report is to be filled out on a standard form, or if the report is one that employees fill out frequently, there's often no need for an introduction, because the information provided at the top of the form tells readers everything that would be in such a topic sentence. A sample report of this type appears later in this chapter.

Body

The paragraphs in the body of the report support the main idea. The more detailed and specific you are in this support, the better. Remember that the body of your report should not evaluate or assess the facts you report. Opinions or impressions should be reserved for the conclusion or recommendations section. (If you need a quick review of reporting strategies, see Chapter 7.)

The body of a report, like the body of a memo, can be made reader-friendly by the use of headings, lists, tables, and graphs.

Save Your Reader's Time

If your report is long or has a large amount of supporting data, you don't need to include all of that data in the report. Instead, *summarize* the data and include the complete data as an attachment or appendix. For example, if you're reporting on all work-related accidents, you might summarize accident data and attach copies of all the accident reports.

Conclusion/Recommendations

The conclusion should tell readers if there is any action to be taken or if there are any recommendations based upon what you've reported. For example, in a progress report, your conclusion might present your goals for the next report period or discuss problems you've been having during this report period. An accident report might recommend changes to be made to prevent similar accidents in the future.

TYPES OF REPORTS

Now let's look at how this report structure works for a few specific types of reports.

Progress Report

Most reports follow a chronological order. A progress report, for example, will begin by naming the time period covered in the report. If it's a long and detailed report, it may also begin with a summary of what has been accomplished. Then the body will be organized as follows:

- *Past:* what has been accomplished
- *Present:* what work is in progress
- *Future:* future plans/goals and a time line for completion

Be specific about what you have accomplished and plan to accomplish. List any issues or concerns that you may have (things that may prevent you from achieving your goals, for example). Read the progress report on the next page as an example.

PROGRESS REPORT

For the week of: 11/13/99–11/20/99
Submitted by: Robert Evans
Department: Facilities

Completed:
- Repaired the damage to the roof from the weekend's ice storm. (This took two full days.)
- Replaced the pipes under the sink in the men's restroom.
- Repaired the cracks in the wall in the 2nd floor Conference Room.
- Replaced lightbulbs in the hallways.

In Progress:
- Painting the cafeteria.

To Do (please rank in order of priority):
- Install the new window blinds in the 3rd floor Conference Room that arrived yesterday.
- Clean up the branches and other debris from the ice storm.
- Continue painting the cafeteria. I had hoped to complete this task by the end of the week, but clean-up from the ice storm took priority. I will probably not finish until the end of next week.

Notice that there's no sentence naming the report period because the report form has a blank for that information. Notice also that the writer doesn't need transitions because of the way the report form divides the sections and because he has used bullets to list the items in his report. In addition, the writer mentions a concern about his ability to complete a certain project on time.

Most reports will follow this same basic structure.

Incident Report

An incident report should be formatted as follows:

- *Past:* what happened
- *Present:* what the situation is now
- *Future:* what might happen or should happen (recommenda-tions/concerns)

For your reference, the incident report from Chapter 7 is reprinted below.

INCIDENT REPORT

Submitted by: <u>Matthew Thomas</u>   Date of Incident: <u>1/21/00</u>
Position: <u>Security Guard, 2nd shift</u> Time of Incident: <u>17 : 18</u>
Date of Report: <u>1/22/00</u>   Location of Incident: <u>Human Resources</u>

Description of Incident:

On Monday, January 22, at 16:32, Mr. R. Turner, a former employee, signed in at the security desk. He exchanged his driver's license for a visitor pass and put his destination down as Human Resources. At 17:18, I received a call from Maria Louis, the assistant director of Human Resources. She asked me to come to Human Resources immediately because Mr. Turner refused to leave the office and she could not lock up. I left Mark Davidson on duty at the desk and reached Human Resources at approximately 17:21. When I arrived, Mr. Turner was sitting by the receptionist's desk. I told Mr. Turner that the office was closed and that he had to leave. He said he would not leave until he saw John Francis, the director of Human Resources. Maria then told me that Mr. Francis was not in that day and that she told Mr. Turner several times that Mr. Francis was not in, but Mr. Turner did not believe her. She said Mr. Turner was waiting because he believed he would catch Mr. Francis as he tried to leave. Then I asked Mr. Turner if this was true, and he said yes. I told him that Mr. Francis was not in and that he could no longer sit in the Human Resources office. If he wished to wait, he could wait by the security desk, but he would be waiting until tomorrow morning. Then I asked Mr. Turner to follow me, and he did. After I escorted him to the security desk, I asked him if he wanted to wait or if he wanted his ID back. He said he'd come back later, so I returned his ID and he signed out at 17:30. Maria had followed us to the security desk, and after Mr. Turner left, she told me that Mr. Turner had just been fired for failing to pass a random drug test.

Trip Report

A trip report should be formatted as follows:

- *Past:* what you did or saw
- *Present:* how you feel about it, how you are using it in your work
- *Future:* how this can be used in your work, other trips, etc.

Meeting Minutes

A report containing minutes of a meeting should generally be formatted as follows:

Heading. Begin your report with the following information:

- the name of the group or meeting
- the date and time of the meeting
- the names of those who attended the meeting
- if this is a group that meets regularly, list the names of those who were absent

Body. Briefly describe each topic discussed during the meeting. For each topic:

- state the issue
- describe the main points and concerns (and who stated them)
- describe the solution or action agreed upon

- list any assignments (who will do what) and deadlines for those assignments

Conclusion. You may conclude with the date and time of the next meeting to be held.

Here's an example:

Employee Advocate Committee
Minutes of the Meeting Held:

July 3, 2000
2:00 P.M.

In Attendance:	Jules Richardson, Chairperson
	Harold VanDyke, Secretary
	Lucinda Real
	Michelle Madden
	Oliver Wilson
	Jason Smith
Absent:	Raul Perez
	Brenda Tilden

1. **Employee Lounge.** Michelle reported that employee complaints about the lounge have increased. Specific complaints include insufficient locker space, insufficient seating, a dirty refrigerator, lack of telephones, and a malfunctioning microwave. Lucinda suggested surveying employees to find out how the lounge could best be redesigned. Michelle and Jason were asked to compose and conduct the survey. Harold suggested putting a suggestion box in the lounge. The committee agreed that a survey would be more systematic and would get more input from more employees. Oliver volunteered to write a proposal for redesigning the lounge based upon that survey. Michelle and Jason will bring a draft of the survey to the next meeting.

2. **Four-Day Work Week.** Harold proposed asking management to allow employees to choose between a five-day work week (8 hours/day) and a four-day work week (10 hours/day). Jason noted that this could create a scheduling nightmare for shift supervisors. Harold agreed to talk with shift supervisors informally about the idea and find out their concerns. He will report on his conversations next week.

3. **Employee Appreciation Day.** Jules reminded the committee that it was time to plan the annual Employee Appreciation Day. Michelle and Lucinda volunteered to come up with several ideas for a theme by next week's meeting.

The committee will reconvene next Monday, July 10, at 2:00 P.M.

PRACTICE

1. Take one of the practice exercises you wrote in Chapter 7 and rewrite it in an official report form.
2. Write a progress report for your work in this book. You can follow the format of the sample listed in this chapter, but this report needs some kind of introduction.

Possible Answers for Practice Exercises

1. Answers will vary. Just make sure you follow the *past, present, future* format.
2. Here's a sample progress report (next page):

PROGRESS REPORT
Submitted by: Robert Evans
Date: 1/2/00

This is a progress report for my studies in *Improve Your Writing for Work*.

- I began with Chapter 1 last Monday. I have done one chapter each day and have now completed Chapters 1–14.
- I am currently working on Chapter 15, which I should finish today.
- I will complete this section (Chapter 18) this week and take the weekend off. Then I will complete the book by doing Chapters 19–23 next week.

Chapters 20 and 21 deal with clarity and style, which I think are my weaknesses, so I plan to pay particular attention to those chapters.

In Short

Reports generally follow a three-part structure that begins with the subject of the report, provides the details of the report, and then concludes with comments or recommendations. Most common workplace reports are organized chronologically.

Skill Building Until Next Time

Your company probably has a variety of report forms for employees to fill out . If possible, get copies of some of those reports and samples of what management considers to be good reports. Look at how each type of report is arranged and see if you can determine what characteristics the good reports have in common.

CHAPTER | 16

When you want to propose a project or idea, you may need to write an official proposal. Proposals combine reporting with convincing. This chapter will show you how.

PROPOSALS

"The bottom-line question from your reader is, 'Will this plan work?'"

Philip C. Kolin

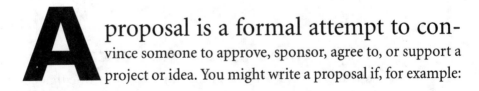A proposal is a formal attempt to convince someone to approve, sponsor, agree to, or support a project or idea. You might write a proposal if, for example:

- You have an idea that will cut your paperwork in half.
- You want to take a few work-related courses at the local community college. Your company doesn't have an official tuition reimbursement policy, but you want the company to pay for your classes.
- You think revising an existing procedure would improve efficiency.

KINDS OF PROPOSALS

There are many different kinds of proposals, and they can range from the very complicated to the very simple. Generally, whatever the kind, proposals fall into one of three categories:

- Proposals to provide goods or services
- Proposals to make a change or improvement
- Proposals to approve a program or project

As an employee, you're most likely to encounter the second type, but the third type is common as well. And some proposals combine purposes. In any case, all proposals, complex or simple, follow this very basic organizational structure:

$$problem \rightarrow solution$$

Any type of proposal must first pose a problem and then offer a solution for it. Your job as a writer is to convince readers to accept or approve of the solution you offer.

PARTS OF A PROPOSAL

Proposals have several parts. Depending upon the length and complexity of the proposal, these parts may or may not be separated as individual sections. Not all parts are applicable for every proposal.

Proposal Format
Discuss a problem and then offer a solution.

Title, Author, Date, Audience

Make sure your proposal has a simple, direct title that conveys the gist of your proposal. What is your proposal about? Then, indicate the date, the author of the proposal, and the receiver. Here's an example:

Proposal to Reorganize Employee Report Forms
Submitted to: Alan Wilson
Submitted by: Lisa Green
Date: February 10, 2000

If you're writing your proposal in memo form, then this information will be taken care of in the heading of your memo, and you should not repeat it in the body.

Problem Statement

Begin your proposal by clearly describing the problem you propose to fix. Be sure to provide sufficient background information so that readers fully understand the problem. For example, if you are proposing a revision of procedures in your department, don't assume that your readers know those procedures. Carefully consider your audience and assess what they do and don't know about the situation. Write for the lowest common denominator of knowledge.

Describe the Solution

After you describe the problem, it's time to describe your solution. First, provide a general topic sentence that summarizes the solution. Then provide the specific details of the solution. You can break the solution down into the following parts:

- procedures
- personnel
- materials
- time line
- budget

Procedures

If your solution requires several steps or complicated procedures, a procedures section will be helpful for readers. List the steps to be taken in chronological order. Readers need to know exactly what's involved in a solution before they can approve it.

Personnel

If several people will be working on this solution, explain who those people are, what exactly they will be doing, and why they'd be the best ones to accomplish those tasks.

Materials

List any special equipment or materials that will be required to implement your solution.

Time Line

How long will your solution take to implement? Can it be done in a day, a week, a year? Offer your best guess. If possible, provide a schedule that lists specific tasks and a date for completion of each of them.

Budget

How much will it cost to implement your solution? If there are large costs involved, it's a good idea to provide a budget. Remember, when convincing, you need to anticipate readers' questions and objections, and one question they're sure to ask is "How much will this cost?" Make sure your budget is accurate; this section can make or break your proposal.

SAMPLE PROPOSAL

Below is an example of a proposal for an idea that was discussed previously—creating a Spanish version of an employee training manual. This employee submitted her proposal on the company's proposal form:

GRAND IDEAS
Marlett Grand Hotel

Submitted by: Maritza Luz
Department/Title: Housekeeping Supervisor
Date: 8/21/00

Please describe your idea below.

As you know, over half of our employees speak Spanish as their native language, and many of them have not had a formal education in English. As a result, many of them have difficulty reading our Employee Training Manual, and I spend much of my time explaining things to employees that they should have learned from reading the manual. Training therefore takes several days longer than it should.

I propose that we translate the manual into Spanish. If we had a version of the manual in their native language, these employees would complete training sooner and have a ready reference throughout their employment. In addition, I wouldn't have to spend as much time telling employees what they should already know.

I am fluent in both English and Spanish and have an excellent command of grammar in both languages. I would be happy to take on this project. I need only a few reference books costing a total of approximately $30, a computer to work on, and approval for overtime hours. I estimate that if I work an extra hour each day for a total of approximately 25 overtime hours, I could have the manual translated in a month for a cost of approximatly $675 (25 hours x $27/overtime hour = $675). Thirty copies of the manual can be printed for approximately $50.

Notice that this proposal includes all of the parts except "procedures," which isn't necessary here.

If this were a more extensive proposal with a lot of details for each part, you could use headings to separate the different parts and use lists and charts wherever possible.

THE GOAL OF A PROPOSAL

Remember that the overall goal of a proposal is to convince. That means you need to:

- Show how your solution will clearly benefit readers
- Anticipate readers' reservations and objections
- Provide specific evidence for your claims

These points were covered in detail in Chapter 12, on the subject of "Convincing" your reader. If you need a quick refresher, spend a few minutes reviewing that chapter.

PRACTICE

Propose an improvement in how employees are treated or trained at your place of work, or propose a way to make something at work more cost effective, less time consuming, or otherwise more efficient and effective. Include all the parts of a proposal that are applicable.

Possible Answer to Practice Exercise

MEMORANDUM

TO: Bob Howard, Payroll Manager
FROM: Alexis Dern, Line Supervisor
DATE: August 4, 1997
RE: Proposal to revise time sheets

Wage-grade employees are currently required to fill out two different time sheets each week: one form for regular hours and a separate form for overtime hours. This means that employees have to write their name, Social Security number, department, supervisor, and week begin/end dates on both sheets and get two supervisor signatures. This is a small but unnecessary waste of time which several employees in my group have complained about.

If the time sheets were combined so that regular and overtime hours can be reported on one form, this would no longer be a problem. Employees could fill out their personal information at the top, their regular hours in the middle, and any overtime hours at the bottom. A combined form would not only save some time each week but it would also save paper. All we need is for someone to design a new form, which should take just a few hours.

IN SHORT

Proposals use the problem–solution format to convince readers to accept a project or idea. They combine reporting and convincing strategies to describe the problem and explain how the solution will be implemented. Your solution can be broken down into these parts: procedures, personnel, materials, timeline, and budget.

Skill Building Until Next Time

Companies that want your business will often send you letters that work like proposals: They address a problem or concern you may have and show how their goods or services could solve that problem for you. Look for such correspondence in the mail over the next couple of days and notice the different parts of the proposal at work.

CHAPTER | 17

The newest form of workplace communication is electronic mail. Fast and efficient, electronic mail is easy to use, but it needs to be used appropriately. This chapter explains how to write effective emails.

ELECTRONIC MAIL

"On the Internet, you exist primarily in the words you write. What you say is who you are in an online world."

Eric Crump and Mick Carbone

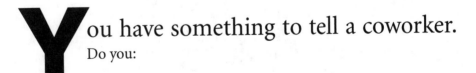

ou have something to tell a coworker. Do you:

- walk to your coworker's office?
- call your coworker?
- send a memo?
- write an email?

The answer, of course, is that it depends upon a number of different factors. Which method you use to communicate will have an impact on how effective your communication is. Electronic mail (email) is a relatively new way to communicate in the workplace, and it has many advantages. The more you know about communicating via email, the more likely you are to use email appropriately and get your message across clearly.

THE NATURE OF EMAIL

Email is something of a cross between a telephone conversation and a memo. Not as "real time" (immediate) as a telephone conversation, it is often a much faster way to transmit a message than the typical memo or letter. Not as interactive as a telephone conversation, it still allows you to reply to someone else's comments and questions. Not as concrete or official as a hard-copy memo, it still serves as a record of communication and can be printed or stored and referred to as necessary. In short, email is a unique medium that allows "conversations" to take place in writing.

While you don't have the advantage of hearing the other person's tone of voice as you would on the telephone, when you write an email, you do have one of the best advantages of the writing process: the time to pause and reflect upon what you write before you send your message.

Email Format

Email messages follow a format very similar to memos. In most email programs, an email message begins with a header that includes the following (the order may vary depending upon your email program):

- Name and address of the sender
- Name(s) and address(es) of the recipient(s) (both direct recipients and cc's)
- Date (and sometimes the time) of the email
- Subject of the email

Beneath this header is the body of the email, which contains the actual message.

Of course, the most basic difference between an email message and a memo is that email messages are electronic—they're written, sent, and read directly on the computer. Because it's harder to read on the computer than on paper, there are two rules that apply if you want your messages to be reader friendly:

1. Keep your messages short
2. Use email only in appropriate situations

When to Use Email

Each writing situation is unique, and you'll have to determine the best means of communicating your message in each individual case. Still, there are some general guidelines that can help you determine whether or not an email message is appropriate. In general, an email message is appropriate in the following situations:

- **The message does not concern legal or other official matters** that require an official hard copy on company letterhead or in an approved memo format.
- **You will have trouble reaching the person** by telephone and you know that the recipient checks email regularly.
- **You want your reader to be able to respond to you at his leisure.**
- **Your message is urgent**, but you can't reach the person by telephone, and you need a response as soon as possible.
- **Your message is short.** Readers want to send and receive messages quickly, and they don't want to spend a lot of time reading messages on their screen. In general, don't send long email messages. If your message is long or complicated—if it's something the reader will have to print out in order to properly read and review—then send a letter or memo or send a brief email message and attach your document to it (a lengthy memo or report, for example).
- **The recipient has expressed a preference for receiving communications via email.** For example, your supervisor may tell you that she would like to receive all meeting minutes via email rather than interoffice memo.

HOW TO WRITE EFFECTIVE EMAILS

The key to writing effective emails can be summed up in this one rule:

> Remember there is a *person* on the receiving end of your message. Always show respect for that person.

Because we write, send, and receive emails on a computer without any human interaction, it can be easy to forget that we're writing to a human being, not a computer screen. It's also easy to imagine that your email will "evaporate" once it's read. But emails can be printed, and (at least in most email systems) they're stored both on your computer and on your recipient's computer, and other people may access and read your emails. Therefore, a second rule also applies:

> Don't say anything in an email that you wouldn't say in print.

Five additional guidelines will help you write effective emails:

- Take the time to write it right
- Be brief
- Use an appropriate level of formality
- Use an appropriate tone
- Keep the format simple

Take the Time to Write It Right

Probably the single most common cause of poor email communication is haste. Because email allows us to send and receive messages so quickly, many people make the mistake of *writing* their messages quickly, too.

When people rush the writing of emails, several problems typically occur. The message may be inaccurate or incomplete; it may be much longer than it should be; it may not have the appropriate level of formality; and it may completely miss the mark in its tone. In addition, it might be full of errors and typos that can confuse your reader.

Although email messages are perceived to be fast and informal, they take just as much time and effort to compose as any other workplace communication. Here are some specific guidelines to help you write effectively:

- **Compose your message carefully.** Treat your email like any other workplace communication. Ask prewriting questions, state your main idea clearly from the beginning, and offer support for that main idea. Be sure to provide any necessary context. Make the subject of your email very clear in the subject line.
- **Read through your message** *at least once* **before you send it.** Make sure it says what you want to say, the way you want to say it.
- **Proofread your message before you send it.** Though email is a more informal medium than letters and memos, that doesn't mean grammar and mechanics (spelling and punctuation) can go by the wayside. Typos and grammatical errors can mean that your communication will be misunderstood. And a sloppy email sends the message that you don't respect your reader enough to proofread. (You'll get to review grammar and mechanics in Chapter 23.)

Be Brief

You know the popular saying: time is money. Well, it's true in cyberspace as well as on paper. To save your readers' time—and minimize the strain on their eyes—**keep your email messages short.** Use shorter sentences and shorter paragraphs than you would in a memo or letter. A typical 6-line paragraph is fine on paper, but if you can break it into two 3-line paragraphs in email, it will be considerably easier to read. Here's an example:

Subject:	**Summer schedule**
Date:	**Monday, May 22, 2000 09:48:02**
From:	**Jane Borowski <jborowski@toolbox.com>**
To:	**Annie Sloan <asloan@toolbox.com>**

Annie, can we meet to review the summer schedule? I'm available every day this week after 11:00.

Please let me know which day/time is good for you.

Thanks,
Jane

Notice that there are only three sentences, and each sentence is short and to the point. In addition, what would be one paragraph in a memo is split into two paragraphs in this email. This breaks up the ideas on the screen and makes the message easier to read.

Use an Appropriate Level of Formality

Memos are typically less formal than letters, and emails—whether they're reporting, convincing, reviewing, proposing or informing—are typically less formal than memos.

Because email often feels like a telephone conversation, it's okay to do what you wouldn't do in a typical letter or memo but what you often do on the telephone: chat. Many effective emails start and/or end with some informal small talk. In fact, in some cases, your recipient might be a little offended if you *don't* include a little personal note. It all depends, of course, upon your relationship with the recipient. Here's the example from above, this time revised to include some chit-chat:

Subject:	**Summer schedule**
Date:	**Monday, May 22, 2000 09:48:02**
From:	**Jane Borowski <jborowski@toolbox.com>**
To:	**Annie Sloan <asloan@toolbox.com>**

Hi, Annie. How was your vacation? I hope you had a wonderful time.

Now that you're back, can we meet to review the summer schedule?

I'm available every day this week after 11:00. Please let me know which day/time is good for you.

Thanks!
Jane

This email opens with a short paragraph asking the recipient about something personal—her recent vacation. In addition, the request to meet is more friendly and informal, starting off with "now that you're back." The exclamation point after "thanks" strengthens the sense of appreciation for the recipient's time. Clearly, the Annie and Jane of this email are much more familiar and friendly with each other than the Annie and Jane of the first version. Here's a version that's even more informal:

Subject:	**Summer schedule**
Date:	**Monday, May 22, 2000 09:48:02**
From:	**Jane Borowski <jborowski@toolbox.com>**
To:	**Annie Sloan <asloan@toolbox.com>**

Welcome back! Can't wait to hear about your vacation.

We need to review the summer schedule.... I'm good after 11 all week. What's good for you?

See you soon,
J

Informal indeed, and just fine, so long as Annie and Jane are very familiar and friendly with each other.

Use an Appropriate Tone

Perhaps the most difficult thing about writing emails is establishing the proper **tone**. Tone is the mood or attitude conveyed by words or speech. For example, consider the word "sure." Depending upon your tone when you say this word, it can have at least half a dozen meanings. In fact, whatever words you use, in speech and in writing, meaning *depends* upon tone. So how can you make sure your reader "hears" the right tone in an email? A few strategies can help.

Choose Your Words Carefully

Writing is all about making choices, and word choice is particularly important in email messages. Imagine, for example, that you have received a poorly written report from someone on your production team. How would you express your dissatisfaction with this report? Notice the range of word choice in the sentences below—and the resulting range of tone in those sentences:

1. Tom, your report was a joke.
2. Tom, your report was AWFUL.
3. Tom, your report was unsatisfactory.
4. Tom, your report did not meet my expectations.
5. Tom, your report needs improvement.

You can see that the messages start angry and insulting and grow progressively gentler in tone. Be selective; choose the word that carries the right tone.

Use Typographical Clues

Typographical clues include **capital letters** and **emoticons**. Writing in ALL CAPITAL LETTERS (like using exclamation points) conveys a strong emotion. Use all capitals (and exclamation points) sparingly. For one thing, words in all capitals are difficult to read. For another, all capitals suggest that you are shouting at your reader. Whether you're shouting in anger or ecstasy, you're still shouting, and it should be kept to a minimum.

Emoticons are an email innovation created to help convey tone. These symbols—keyboard variations of the smiley face—serve as substitutes for the facial expressions you cannot see and tone of voice you cannot hear. The table below lists a few of the most common emoticons. For a more extensive list, visit the website http://wellweb.com/behappy/smiley.htm.

Emoticon	Approximate Meaning
:-)	I'm happy.
:-(	I'm sad.
;-)	Said slyly, with a wink, tongue-in-cheek.
:-@	I'm screaming.
:-o	Uh-oh!

Naturally, emoticons should *not* be used in formal emails, like an email to the entire company regarding a change in policy. Reserve them for when you have a very informal, friendly relationship with the recipient.

Review Carefully

Before you send an email, read it carefully and objectively. How does it sound? If you're at all concerned that you haven't established the proper tone—if you think it might sound a little too angry, whiny, desperate, whatever—have someone else read it. In addition, before you send your message, ask yourself two questions:

1. Would you say what you've written to the recipient's face?
2. Would you feel uncomfortable if what you've written were circulated in a printed memo?

If you answer yes to either of these questions, you should revise your message.

Keep the Format Simple

When you write a letter, memo, report, proposal, or any other workplace document, you generally have the ability to format your document so that it's easy to read. But in an email, formatting can be problematic; one email system might not be able to translate the formatting of a message from another system. As a result, the headings, lists, tables and other formatting features of your document are likely to be lost.

That doesn't mean, however, that you should abandon readability strategies. Instead, adapt them to the electronic environment as follows:

Headings

Don't use boldfacing, underlining, or different fonts for headings in your email. Instead, to indicate a heading, type the word or phrase on a line by itself (white space before and after). You can indicate levels of headings by putting LEVEL 1 HEADINGS in all capitals, Level 2 Headings in initial capitals, and Level 3 headings in sentence capitals.

Lists

Don't use bullets in your lists. Instead, use asterisks (*), dashes (–), numbers, or letters. If any items in your list are more than one line long, to help distinguish between items, put a space between them.

Tables and Graphs

Avoid tables and graphs in email; most formatting features will be tangled or lost in translation. Whenever possible, summarize the information that is in the table or graph, and include the complete table or graph as an attachment.

PRACTICE

1. Revise the following draft so that it is appropriate for an email.

   Joel—You missed our department meeting AGAIN. DUH!! Don't you have a calendar? Go out and buy yourself one and WRITE DOWN OUR MEETING DATES AND TIMES. Or maybe you forgot how to get to the meeting room. It's down the hall from Eileen's office, remember? Room 331. BE THERE NEXT WEEK. Get the minutes from Eileen.
   —ED

2. You're the assistant to the office manager. Next Saturday, a carpet company is coming in to install new carpets. Everything except furniture must be removed from the floor, and all items except for computers and telephones must be removed from on top of furniture by the end of the business day on Friday. It is very important to get everyone's cooperation. Write an email to all employees asking them to prepare their offices accordingly.

Possible Answers to Practice Exercises

1. The main problem with this email is its tone. It is much too angry and insulting. Here's a more professional yet still suitably informal email:

   Joel: You missed our department meeting for the third time this month.

   Please remember that we meet every Tuesday at 8:30 a.m. in Room 331. Your attendance is important and expected. If there's some difficulty keeping you from these meetings, please let me know. Otherwise, I look forward to seeing you next Tuesday.

Eileen has minutes from yesterday's meeting. Please pick them up from her as soon as possible. Thanks.

Ed

2. Answers will vary. Here's one possibility:

Subject: Carpet Installation
Date: Monday, May 22, 2000 09:48:02
From: Jane Borowski <jborowski@toolbox.com>
To: All Employees <group@toolbox.com>

ATTENTION

This Saturday, May 27, Under-Your-Feet Carpet Company will be installing new carpets throughout the building. To prepare for this installation, by 5:00 p.m. on Friday, please:

1. Remove ALL non-furniture items from the carpet of your work area.

2. Remove ALL items except computers and telephones from the top of your furniture.

Your compliance is very important. I will send a reminder on Thursday and again on Friday morning. Thank you in advance for your cooperation.

If you have any questions, please don't hesitate to contact me at x3321.

Thank you,

Jane

P.S. For those of you who are wondering … the new carpeting is light blue. I have samples in my office if you'd like to take a look.

IN SHORT

Use email only in appropriate situations and try to keep your messages brief. Taking the time to compose and proofread your email carefully will help you choose an appropriate level of formality and achieve the right tone. Be careful not to say anything in an email that you wouldn't want to see in print.

Skill Building Until Next Time

Examine the email messages you receive this week. How effective are they? Notice the difference between long and short emails—which ones do you prefer to read? How formal are the messages? See if you can spot any typographical clues in them.

CHAPTER | 18

The newest kind of
workplace writing is
taking place online. But
writing for the web
requires some special
strategies. This chapter
explains how to organize
information for a web
site and how to write
effective text for
the web.

WEBSITES

*"The success of a traditional website is measured by
how many visitors come and come back. That is not
[our] goal... The success of [our] documents ... is
measured by how many readers find what they need
quickly, how useful they find the document, and how
efficient it is."*

Dan Bricklin

Whether you surf the Internet every
chance you get or you don't even know what "surfing the
Internet" means, one thing is clear: more and more companies are posting their products and services on the World Wide Web.
For many businesses, continued success may soon depend upon a strong
presence in this new medium. And as many companies develop web strategies, more and more workplace writing will be destined for the web.

WHAT IS A WEBSITE?
Websites are electronic documents located on the **World Wide Web**
(**WWW**). The WWW is a network of documents linked together through

the **Internet**, itself a giant "network of networks" that connects computer users around the globe. Websites generally have five components:

- **Text:** The written information on the site.
- **Navigation:** How that information is organized.
- **Graphics:** The pictures, tables, graphs, and other visuals on the site.
- **Design:** The look and feel of the site, determined by colors, font, and the layout of text and graphics.
- **Special effects:** Animation, sound, video, and other multimedia effects.

In this chapter, you'll learn about the first two components: navigation and text. No matter how visually appealing a website may be, it's not a good website if it doesn't clearly and effectively communicate the kind of information users need.

Websites, Web Pages, and Hypertext

A **website** is actually a collection of individual web **pages** much like a book is a collection of individual chapters. The key difference is that most books are meant to be read linearly, from start to finish, chapter by chapter and page by page. Websites, however, don't follow this traditional narrative pattern. Like "choose your own adventure" books, in a website, visitors choose how they want to move around among the pages. This **hypertext** format allows readers to jump back and forth and cross reference information. Visitors "jump" by clicking the mouse on hypertext **links** that move them from page to page. Exactly how readers are able to move around among the pages is determined by the navigation of the site.

In a website, some pages are accessible from any screen. For example, in most websites, no matter where you are, you can always click on a link to return to the **home page** (the title page or starting point) of the site. Other pages, however, are only accessible from particular pages. For example, if you are at a camera shop's website, you may only be able to link to the page "Choosing Your Camera Lens" from the "Accessories" page.

If you are writing content for a website, you have to decide what information will be available from each page within your website and how visitors can move about among your pages. The best way to do this is to create a site map.

CREATING A SITE MAP

A **site map** allows you to determine exactly how your information will be organized. Which information will visitors get first? How many clicks will it take for your reader to find a certain piece of information? A site map plans the paths visitors may take and helps you arrange the hierarchy of information and links within your site.

To develop a site map:

1. **First, determine your audience and purpose.** Who do you expect to visit your site? Who do you *want* to visit your site? Why will they come? What do you want them to do as a result of visiting your site?

2. Based upon your audience and purpose, **determine the information you want to include.** Break that information into as many small chunks as possible.

3. **Arrange your information hierarchically, with the most important information first.** Information on a website should be organized much like a newspaper article, which provides the most essential information (the *who, what, when, where, why,* and *how*) right from the beginning. This is simply a matter of being reader friendly and being business savvy. If your readers have to click ten times before they find out what services your company provides, chances are you'll lose lots of those readers long before that tenth click.

Your first level of pages should contain the most important information; the second level, the secondary information; the third level, the tertiary information; and so on. The deeper your visitors get into the site, the less important (the more detailed, less "big picture") the information should be.

Organizing Your Information

As an example, let's look at how Stuart Liddel developed a website for his company, Stuart Liddel's Animal Kind Rodent Removal Service. To create a site map for his website, Stuart began by clarifying his audience and purpose:

Audience: People who are looking for a rodent removal service but don't want to kill the animals.

Purpose: To explain our approach to rodent removal, describe our services, and get our audience's business.

Then, Stuart decided which information to include. First he determined the main categories of information he wanted on the site. Then he clarified his purpose for each category:

Category	Purpose
Company History	To describe when we got started, where, and why, and to describe how we've been doing over the years; to give people a feel for what kind of people are behind this company.
Company Philosophy	To explain our approach to rodent removal and why we don't use poison or other harmful techniques; to show that we respect all animal life; and to show how this approach is not only as good as, but better than, conventional approaches.
Services	To describe the services we offer.
Frequently Asked Questions	To help people quickly find answers to the most common questions about rodent removal and our company.
Rodent Encyclopedia	To help people better understand rodents, why they infest, and why these animals deserve the same respect as other animals.
Contact Us	To tell people how to contact us.

Then, under each of these headings, Stuart decided what specific information to include in each section and divided that information into chunks:

Company History	Company Philosophy	Services	Frequently Asked Questions	Rodent Encyclopedia	Contact Us
• when and why we began • how we've grown	• respect all animal life • traps, not poison	• inspection • removal • prevention	1. what attracts rodents? 2. why traps instead of poison? 3. what kind of traps do you use? 4. what do you do with the rodents you trap? 5. how can I prevent rodent infestation?	• all about mice • all about rats • all about chipmunks and squirrels • all about groundhogs	• address • phone number • fax number • email address

Finally, Stuart checked each of *these* categories of information to see if they could be broken down into even smaller chunks. In the "Services" column, he decided that under "prevention," he would have two sections: "seminar" and "monthly maintenance." For his Rodent Encyclopedia, he decided to include information about "nesting," "feeding," and "signs of infestation" for each animal. Thus, he added these smaller chunks of information to his web content:

Services	Rodent Encyclopedia
• inspection	• all about mice
• removal	• nesting
• prevention:	• feeding
• seminar	• signs of infestation
• monthly maintenance	• all about rats
	• nesting
	• feeding
	• signs of infestation
	• all about chipmunks and squirrels
	• nesting
	• feeding
	• signs of infestation
	• all about groundhogs
	• nesting
	• feeding
	• signs of infestation

Stuart has decided what he wants to include on his site, and he's organized that information into manageable chunks. Now he's ready to create the actual site map, a "flow chart" that will show how visitors to his site can move to and from each chunk of information.

Navigation Bar

The first item in a site map is the **navigation bar**. This "bar" is like a table of contents for the site. It lists the major divisions of the website and provides links to each of those major sections so that no matter where they are in the site, visitors can always get to those key pages. Stuart decided that his navigation bar would list each of his six main categories (next page).

Home Page

Websites start from a home page which typically tells readers whose site it is; provides the most essential information about that company, person, or organization; and presents the navigation bar. This home page and navigation bar provide the core of a site map. To create your site map, start from the home page and draw a link to each category in your navigation bar. All other pages should flow from these categories. Here's an example of a very basic home page:

Stuart Liddel's

ANIMAL KIND
Rodent Removal Service

318 Freedom Drive
Charleston, WV 11111
(123) 456-7890
stuartliddel@animalkind.com

✵Rodent removal that's kind to your home—and to the animals.✵

| Home | Company History | Company Philosophy | Services | FAQ | Rodent Encyclopedia | Contact Us |

For Animal Kind, Stuart mapped out each chunk of information under its respective category and noted any special links that would connect a particular page to another part of the site. Thus, for each category, he determined which chunk would come in what order—in other words, how a visitor can move throughout the site. On the next page, see the site map he created.

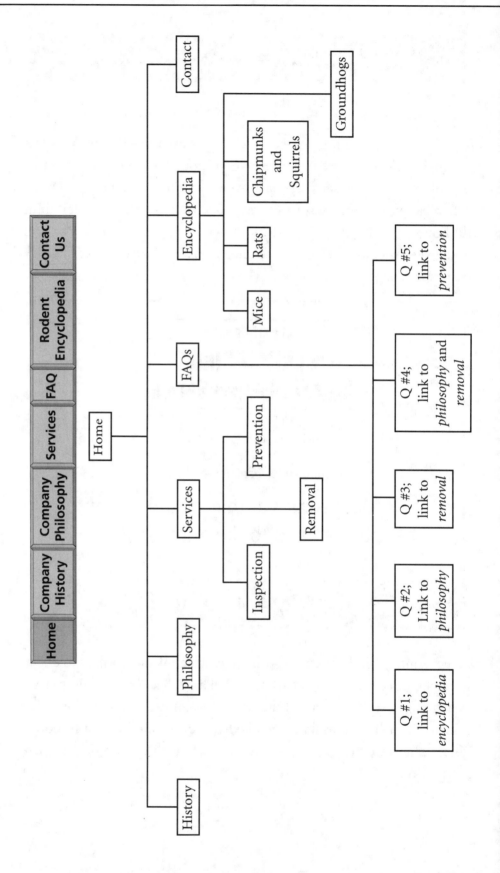

FILLING IN THE TEXT

Once you've created a site map, you can start writing the text. Before you begin, though, it's important to understand how people read text on the web. As visitors are searching for information, they do a lot of **scanning**. When they find the information they're looking for, then they read more carefully. Thus, when writing for the web, your goal should be to help readers find the information they're looking for quickly and easily. Here's how:

Guidelines for Writing Web Text

1. **Break the text into small chunks.** You should already have small chunks from creating your site map. If the information for one chunk is more than a few paragraphs long, be sure to divide that information into additional chunks.

2. **Provide as many headings as possible.**

3. **Limit the number of chunks per page** so that readers can avoid scrolling (moving up and down the screen).

4. **Keep your text short** by writing short sentences and paragraphs. The shorter, the better. In fact, some web experts recommend using half the words you'd use in a paper communication.

5. **Use lots of lists, tables, and graphs.** If you can change text into a list, table, or graph, do it. The more visually you present information in this medium, the better.

6. **Highlight key words and phrases** so that they're easy for the scanning eye to see.

7. **Use an appropriate level of formality.** Like email, the web is a somewhat less formal medium than printed text. Websites that show a personal touch and a little personality are often more effective than those that don't.

8. **Revise and proofread carefully.** Like any other workplace communication, text that appears on the web says a great deal about you, your company, and how much you care about your readers. Make sure your communication is clear and correct.

Here, for example, is the text Stuart wrote for his "Company History" page. Notice how he divided the information into small chunks, used headings, and stuck to short sentences and paragraphs. Notice also his personal, story-telling tone and the way he highlights two key phrases: "humane removal" and "rodent-free homes."

Stuart Liddel's
ANIMAL KIND
Rodent Removal Service

Company History

How It All Began

One morning in 1980, I woke up to a scream: my daughter had seen a mouse in the kitchen. We soon discovered a large family of mice living in our basement. I wanted to get the mice out of the house, but I didn't want to kill them. I'd had all kinds of pets as a kid—mice and rats as well as tarantulas and bats. I have always believed that *every animal has a right to life*.

But no exterminator would remove the mice without poison or deadly traps. So I decided to catch them myself, with live animal traps, and then set them free in the neighboring state park. It was easy, fast, and cheap, and I felt great about it. And I knew there had to be others out there who would prefer **humane removal** to extermination. A few months later, Stuart Liddel's Animal Kind Rodent Removal Service was born.

Twenty Years of Service

Since then, Animal Kind has grown from a one-man operation in the basement of our Charleston home to a solid company with 24 full-time employees and over 1200 satisfied clients. The majority of our new customers have heard about us through fellow animal lovers who are enjoying their **rodent-free homes.**

| Home | Company History | Company Philosophy | Services | FAQ | Rodent Encyclopedia | Contact Us |

PRACTICE

Choose an item or service with which you are very familiar. Then, imagine you own a small shop selling that good or service and you want to create a website for your store. First, create a site map. What are the chunks of information? How should they be organized? Then, write the text for one of those chunks.

Possible Answer to Practice Exercise

Answers will vary, of course. On the next page is a sample site map for a website about interior painting. On the page after the site map is text for one of the pages, "Prepping the Walls."

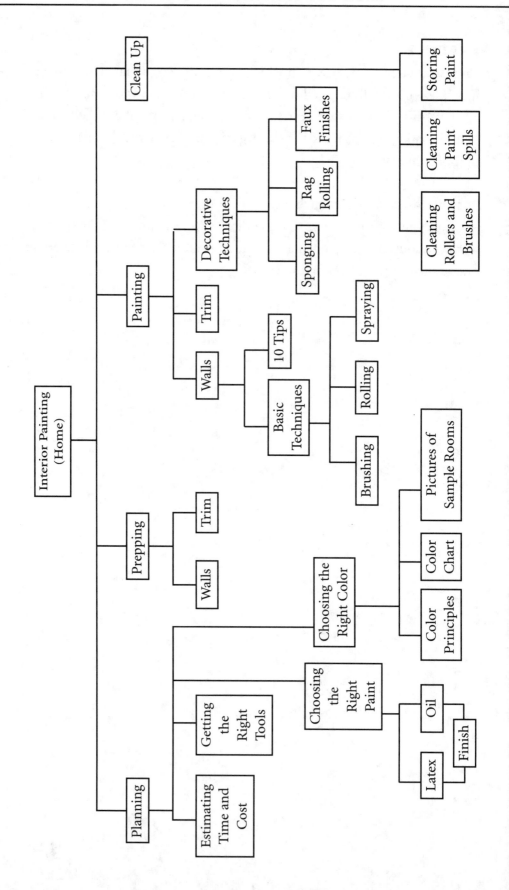

PREPPING THE WALLS

For a smooth, even finish, you must properly prepare the walls for paint. Here's how:

STEP 1: WASH Mix powdered household detergent and water and scrub walls to remove dirt, oil, and stains. Rinse thoroughly. Allow walls to dry completely.

STEP 2: SPACKLE Use spackle to fill in any nicks, holes, or dips in the walls. Allow spackle to dry thoroughly.

STEP 3: SAND Sand walls with a fine grade sandpaper on a pole sander or sanding block. Make sure walls are smooth and even. Wipe walls clean with a tack cloth.

STEP 4: PRIME Unless you're painting walls the same color, apply at least one coat of **primer**, especially on bare wood and spackled areas. Primer will:

- hide stains and darker colors
- seal porous surfaces
- level out uneven surfaces
- "anchor" the paint for a smooth, even finish

Allow primer to dry thoroughly before applying your selected color.

HOME | PLANNING | PREPPING | PAINTING | CLEAN UP

IN SHORT

Writing for the web requires special organization and writing strategies. Carefully consider your audience and purpose and then create a site map that organizes information hierarchically, from most important to least important. Keep your text short and use as many readability strategies as possible to help readers who are scanning the text.

Skill Building Until Next Time

Spend some time surfing the World Wide Web. Find sites that are effectively organized and well written and others that aren't. Notice what the good sites do well that the others don't. You will probably find lots of sites that *look* good but that don't organize and present their information effectively.

SECTION 4

TIPS FOR AN EASY READ

The previous sections have shown you ways to develop, organize, and format your ideas. This section focuses on how to clearly and concisely express those ideas and make sure your writing is smooth and effective. In these five chapters, you'll learn how to:

- Write effective introductions and conclusions
- Write clearly
- Write with an appropriate style
- Revise
- Edit

The chapters in this section also aim to pull together all that you've learned so far, so your workplace communications are polished and effective.

CHAPTER | 19

Writers often get stuck on introductions and conclusions. This chapter will give you strategies and standard introductory and concluding phrases you can use to eliminate writer's block for these key areas.

INTRODUCTIONS AND CONCLUSIONS

"The reader has a right to know, as early on as possible, what a communication is about."

Jefferson Bates

For many writers, introductions and conclusions are the most difficult writing tasks. However, if you're armed with specific strategies for writing introductions and conclusions, you'll be able to all but eliminate this problem.

INTRODUCTIONS

The first piece of advice about introductions may surprise you. If you find yourself unable to write because you don't know how to get started, *skip the introduction*. Sometimes it's easier to get to the meat of what you're writing than to think of the perfect opening sentence. This doesn't mean you shouldn't have your purpose clearly in mind; it just means you should get something written and then come back later to the section that had you stuck.

Even if you use this strategy, of course, you still have to write the introduction eventually. This will be easier if you know exactly what belongs in an introduction and what introductions should do. In general, introductions should:

1. Tell readers what the communication is about (the subject).
2. Tell readers what you think, feel, or know about that subject (the main idea).

And sometimes introductions should also:

3. Catch the reader's attention.

Begin with a Clear Topic Sentence

Although it's been mentioned before, it bears repeating: When you're writing for work, one of the easiest and, in fact, best ways to begin is with a topic sentence that clearly states your purpose. This means you have to do some prewriting to clarify your purpose.

Here is a section reprinted from Chapter 3. Notice how the writer develops a topic sentence from the prewriting questions:

Topic:	new uniform policy
Audience:	all employees in production department
Purpose:	inform employees about the new uniform policy and when it begins
Topic sentence:	A new dress code for all employees will go into effect beginning on the first of the month.

In just about anything you write for work, you can use a topic sentence as an introduction. It's clear, straightforward, and right to the point. And it fulfills one of the underlying rules for workplace writing: respecting the reader's time.

Use Standard Introductory Phrases

Another option is to use standard introductory phrases. Most of these are actually variations of purpose statements, but because they've been used so often, they've become "standard." Here's a list of some of those standard introductory phrases. Feel free to use them, especially if you're stuck:

- It was a pleasure meeting/speaking with you . . .
- Thank you for . . .
- I am writing in response to . . .
- I am writing in regard to . . .
- I am writing to . . .
- As per your request . . .
- This is a reminder that . . .
- I am sorry to report/learn/hear . . .
- I am pleased to inform you . . .
- I regret to inform you . . .

Here are a few examples of complete introductory sentences that use one of these standard phrases:

As per your request, I have completed an inventory of all equipment and supplies in the shipping room.

I am writing to request that the broken oscillating fan in the shipping and receiving office be replaced as soon as possible.

Thank you for your recent application for the position of data processor.

Grab the Reader's Attention

Some proposals, letters, and memos require a different approach, and here's where that third item, catching the reader's attention, comes in. If your subject is something that is not related to official business (such as a company picnic) or something that may "get lost in the crowd," you may benefit from a catchy introduction. For example, remember Jennifer's memo trying to convince her coworkers to participate in the 5K run/walk for the Children's Hospital? Let's look once more at how she introduced that memo:

> **Time is money—and your time could mean money that's desperately needed for important medical research and services.** I'm writing to ask for your time. As you may know, I volunteer at the Children's Hospital. Next month, the hospital is sponsoring a 5K run/walk. Will you participate? We need runners and walkers as well as volunteers to cover registration and t-shirt distribution. The run/walk is on Sunday, May 10, and starts at 9 a.m. If you'd like to participate, please call me at x3035. The registration deadline for participation is April 20. Please help us help children.

Notice how this introduction stands out because it's different from standard purpose-statement introductions. Catchy introductions use a variety of strategies to get readers' attention. They can:

- appeal to readers' needs
- ask questions
- use quotations
- play upon familiar phrases
- state a surprising or shocking fact

For example, here's another catchy introduction that could be used to begin this memo:

> What if you could make a terminally ill child happy? What if you could help a sick child get better?

And another:

> Run! Walk! Help! We need volunteers . . .

Catchy introductions can be very effective in getting your readers' attention, but they should be used only in appropriate situations. Informal writing to coworkers would be an appropriate situation, but in a more official memo to your supervisor about a disciplinary matter, for example, this kind of introduction would not do. Most reports, for example, should not begin with this kind of introduction. It's best reserved for the most informal workplace writing situations and for sales pitches.

PRACTICE A
Write a catchy introduction to a memo responding to Jennifer's request.

CONCLUSIONS
So you've finished the body of a letter, memo, email, or report. Now what? How do you end it? What makes a good conclusion?

When you're writing for work, a good conclusion is usually one that either *looks back* by returning to the topic sentence, or one that *looks forward* to something the reader should do or something the writer expects.

Concluding Strategies
There are a number of ways you can look forward or back, and many of the examples below include standard concluding phrases. You'll see some examples after each strategy to show you how it works. Keep in mind that using one strategy doesn't mean you can't also use another. Good conclusions often use two or three of these strategies together.

1. **Summarize or restate the main idea.** This works best with longer texts.

   Once again, thank you for your help.

   As you can see, a simple time limit would alleviate the problem.

2. **Make a recommendation.** This is a particularly useful conclusion for reports.

   Going forward, I think we should keep track of ...

   TechCom appears to have the best product and service warranty. I suggest we purchase 2 units immediately.

3. **Look to the future.** What do you look forward to doing or accomplishing?

   I look forward to working with you on this project.

   I expect to complete this inventory by Thursday.

4. **Use a call to action.** Tell your readers what they should do.

   Call Ximena by no later than Tuesday, August 1, if you will attend.

   Please respond by Friday, January 16.

   Please fill out the attached form and return it as soon as possible.

5. **Provide a reference person** for readers to contact with questions or for more information.

   If you have any questions, please don't hesitate to call me at extension 333.

   Please call AnneMarie in Accounting for more information.

6. **Thank your readers** for their time or for what you're asking them to do.

   Thank you for your prompt attention to this matter.

   Thank you for your time.

   I appreciate your time and effort.

7. **Remind readers** why this matter is important to them.

   Remember, we cannot process your overtime sheets without a supervisor's signature.

   Your application must be received by Thursday or you will not be considered for the position.

PRACTICE B

Go back to three communications you've written for other exercises and write a different conclusion for each. Try to use three different strategies from the list above.

Possible Answers to Practice Exercises
Practice A

1. I am writing in response to your memo about the Children's Hospital 5K run/walk.
2. Okay! Okay! I will! I'd love to participate.

Practice B

These are three new conclusions for the memo regarding the results of the 5K run/walk in Chapter 14:

1. Without successful fundraisers, the Children's Hospital could not provide the high quality care our precious patients need. Thank you for your help.
2. I look forward to an even more successful fundraiser next year.
3. For next year, I suggest we expand our radio advertising and direct call campaigns. More companies participating means more walkers and more dollars to support our services.

IN SHORT

Introductions and conclusions don't have to be a stumbling block. You can turn your purpose into an opening sentence or choose from several standard introductory and concluding phrases covered in this chapter. For very informal communications, try an introduction that catches the reader's attention.

Skill Building Until Next Time

Sales pitches that you receive in the mail often make use of catchy introductions and powerful conclusions. Other mail you receive will often rely on standard introductory and concluding phrases. Look for these approaches as you read your mail this week.

CHAPTER | 20

Effective writers never forget they're writing for a reader, and they make sure that all of their ideas come across clearly so there's no potential for confusion. This chapter describes practical ways to write more clearly in all your workplace communications.

WRITING CLEARLY

"The difference between the right word and the nearly right word is the same as the difference between lightning and the lightning bug."

Mark Twain

Your workplace communication may have a good introduction and conclusion, but that doesn't mean it's an effective communication—yet. It's now time to make sure that your entire content is written clearly. Otherwise, you might end up with sentences like this:

Because of the fact that this important chapter is of great significance, please hearken and take cognizance of the material that is herein presented within the pages included in this chapter.

Translation: *This chapter is important, so please pay attention.*

If only everything you read for work could be as clear and concise as this translation! Unfortunately, all too often it's not—and instead of clear, simple sentences like the one in this translation, you get confusing, roundabout, wordy, waste-of-my-time sentences like the one shown above. In a word, gobbledygook.

Four rules will help you avoid writing gobbledygook:

1.   **Be clear.**
2.   **Be concise.**
3.   **Use the right degree of formality.**
4.   **Get straight to your point.**

This chapter covers rule 1. Rules 2–4 will be covered in the next chapter, *Writing with Style.* An entire chapter is devoted to this first rule because clarity is absolutely essential for effective workplace communications. After all, if your reader can't understand what you've written, how can you achieve your purpose? You can't. The following strategies will help you write clearly:

- avoid jargon
- avoid pretentious language
- avoid ambiguous language
- avoid unclear pronoun references
- use the active voice

AVOID JARGON

One of the most common flaws in workplace writing is the use of jargon. **Jargon** is technical or specialized language used by a limited audience. For example, you may know what an *adz* is, but unless your readers have had some experience with carpentry or woodwork, chances are *they* don't know. (It's a type of ax used for trimming or shaping wood.) Or you may know what the instructions *"Change to a sans serif font"* mean, but unless your readers have some background in typography or layout, they probably won't. (A

Writing with Clarity
Clarity is the quality of being clear.

sans serif font is a type style that doesn't have small lines finishing off the strokes in the letters. This is a <u>serif</u> font; this is a <u>sans serif</u> font.)

The key to avoiding jargon is to be sure that you write at the appropriate level for your readers. This is why it's so important to know who your readers are. Will they understand you if you use technical language? If you're an electrician and you're writing to other electricians, sure. But if you're an electrician and you're writing to someone in accounting, for example, you'll confuse your reader if you use electrician jargon.

If you must use jargon and your audience is not technical or won't be familiar with your specialized terms, then be sure to *define those terms* for your readers as in the following example:

> Before painting the mullions (the wooden or metal bars between the panes of the window), line the edges of the panes with tape.

This is also true of abbreviations. If you use an abbreviation readers may not know, be sure to define it:

> The wages on the PS (Postal Service) Schedule are different from the wages on the MH (Mail Handler) Schedule.

PRACTICE A

Read the following passages from the chapter entitled "Wage Grade Occupations in Federal Service" in the book *Working for Your Uncle: The Complete Guide to Finding a Job With the Federal Government* (Ossining, NY: Breakthrough Publications, 1993). Are they too technical for a general (non-technical, non-specialized) audience? (Answers to this and the following practice exercises are at the end of the chapter.)

1. **Coin/Currency Checking**

   > This occupation includes jobs involved in visually examining (1) finished coins and medals for finish, appearance, discoloration, missing letters, etc., or (2) U.S. currency, stamps, bonds, and other paper security documents to detect imperfections.

2. Toolmaking

This occupation includes jobs involved in the fabrication, man-
ufacture, calibration, reconditioning, and repair of machine
tools, jigs, fixtures, dies, punches, and gauges used in the man-
ufacture, overhaul, and repair of equipment.

AVOID PRETENTIOUS LANGUAGE

Using pompous or **pretentious language** is another matter. This is a common error because inexperienced writers often believe that big words
impress readers. Listen carefully: They don't. It's *clear writing* that impresses
readers. Sometimes a big, multi-syllable word is the one that most clearly
expresses the idea you want to convey, and that's fine. But there's no need
for a sentence like the following:

Pretentious:	I perambulated the circumference of the room.
Plain English:	I walked around the room.

or like this:

Pretentious:	Engaging my cognitive facilities, I ruminated upon the matter.
Plain English:	I thought about it.

Similarly, there's no need to use words like *utilize* or *facilitate*—*use* and
help are just fine, and often clearer. You don't add any authority or value
to what you write by using big words when short, simple, clear words
will do.

Remember that clarity comes first, and simple, clear words at the right
level of technicality for your reader will help you write clearly.

PRACTICE B

Rewrite the following sentences to eliminate pretentious language. (Use a
dictionary to look up unfamiliar words.)

1. The remuneration you've proposed is incommensurate with my experience with the erection of edifices.

2. I am most beholden to you for your assistance in the furtherance of my cause.

AVOID AMBIGUOUS LANGUAGE

Ambiguous means having two or more possible meanings. So of course ambiguous words and phrases also interfere with clarity. Take a look at this sentence, for example:

The photographer shot the model.

Notice that this sentence can be read two ways: Photographers "shoot" pictures with a camera, but this sentence can also mean that the photographer shot the model with a gun, not with a camera. This kind of ambiguity happens whenever a word has more than one possible meaning by the way it's used in a sentence. You can eliminate the ambiguity in this sentence by revising as follows:

The photographer *took pictures of* the model.

"Took pictures" isn't as powerful a verb as "shot," but at least there's no ambiguity.

Another type of ambiguity happens when a series of words is in the wrong place in a sentence. For example, look at the following sentence:

The woman ate the sandwich with a blue hat.

Here, the *word order* of the sentence, not an individual word, causes the confusion. Did the woman eat her sandwich with her hat? That's what the sentence actually says, but of course that's not what the writer intended. Because the phrase *with a blue hat* is in the wrong place, the sentence becomes unclear. This sentence should be revised to read:

The woman *with a blue hat* ate a sandwich.

Here's another ambiguous sentence:

> While in a meeting, Kerry interrupted her boss.

Because "while in a meeting" is in the wrong place, it's unclear whether Kerry was in a meeting and interrupted her boss or whether Kerry interrupted her boss during her meeting, or whether Kerry and her boss were in the same meeting when Kerry interrupted. Here's one way to revise:

> During their meeting, Kerry interrupted her boss.

PRACTICE C
Eliminate any ambiguity in the following sentences.

1. The famous artist drew stares when he entered the room.
2. I went to see the doctor with a severe headache.

AVOID UNCLEAR PRONOUN REFERENCES
A third item that interferes with clarity is unclear pronoun references. (Pronouns, remember, are words like *me, you, he, she,* etc. that replace nouns.) Here's an example of an unclear pronoun reference:

> I went to the meeting with Ted and Fred, and we took his car.

Whose car? "His" could mean either Ted's or Fred's. Perhaps only Fred has a car, so the writer thought there was no need to explain that it was Fred's car. But remember that your reader may not know what you know, and it's dangerous to assume otherwise. In fact, it's best *never* to *assume* your reader knows background information that you know. This way you won't make the mistake of leaving out information your reader may need.

Here's another example of an unclear pronoun reference:

> It's been years since they tore down that building.

This is an example of a common pronoun error: using a vague "they" when there are specific people behind an action. You may not know who those people are, but you know enough to say something like the following:

It's been years since *a demolition crew* tore down that building.

Here's another example of a vague "they":

Vague: *They* passed a new tax law yesterday.
Clear: *The State Senate* passed a new tax law yesterday.

Be careful of this vague "they." There are always people behind their actions, and your sentences should say so.

PRACTICE D

Eliminate unclear pronoun references from the following sentences.

1. Mr. Jones told Mr. James that he had found his missing report.
2. They closed the movie theater after they discovered several fire code violations.
3. The police officer arrested the man after he attacked a sales clerk.

USE THE ACTIVE VOICE WHEN POSSIBLE

Using the *active voice* means making sure a sentence has a clear agent of action and a direct approach. For example, compare the following sentences:

Passive: The file was put in the wrong drawer.
Active: Someone put the file in the wrong drawer.

Notice how the active sentence gives readers an agent of action—a subject performing a verb. In the passive sentence, you don't know who or what put the file in the wrong drawer; you just know that somehow it got there. The active sentence doesn't name that "someone," but it does provide an agent of action, and as a result it is a more direct sentence.

The active voice also makes a sentence sound more authoritative and powerful—*someone* is doing *something*. In a passive sentence, someone or something has something done to it.

There are times when the passive voice makes more sense than the active—like when you don't know the agent of action or when you want to emphasize the *action*, not the *agent*. The passive voice is also useful when you desire anonymity or objectivity. Here are two examples:

- *The location was deemed suitable by the committee.* (Here, the passive voice emphasizes the *action* of the committee rather than the committee).
- *He was fired.* (The passive voice provides anonymity by not giving an agent of action. Thus, no one has to take the blame for firing him.)

PRACTICE E

Make the following sentences more direct by turning the passive voice into the active.

1.   Protective gear must be worn by all employees when entering the honeycomb area.
2.   The new policy was described by Ms. Wynn at the meeting.
3.   Four months of on-the-job training were completed by the new employees.

Possible Answers to Practice Exercises
Practice A

1.   This is probably not too technical.
2.   This is too technical because the words are too difficult for general readers to understand.

Practice B

1.   The salary you've offered is incommensurate with my construction experience. (Here, the word *incommensurate* is just fine; it's precisely the right word for this sentence.)
2.   I am grateful for your assistance.

Practice C

1.   People stared at the famous artist when he entered the room.
2.   I went to see the doctor about my severe headache.

Practice D

1. Mr. Jones told Mr. James that he had found James' missing report.
2. The fire inspector closed the movie theater down after a local citizen discovered several fire code violations.
3. The police officer arrested the man who had attacked a sales clerk.

Practice E

1. All employees must wear protective gear when entering the honeycomb area.
2. Ms. Wynn described the new policy at the meeting.
3. The new employees completed four months of on-the-job training.

In Short

Clarity is essential for effective workplace writing. Avoid jargon, pretentious language, ambiguity, and unclear pronoun references, and make sure most sentences have a direct agent of action.

Skill Building Until Next Time

Watch for examples of jargon, pretentious language, ambiguity, and unclear pronoun references and the passive voice in the things you read this week. How would you revise those sentences?

CHAPTER | 21

This chapter focuses on workplace writing style. Specifically, these three rules are covered: being concise, using the appropriate level of formality, and getting straight to the point.

WRITING WITH STYLE

"Executives at every level are prisoners of the notion that a simple style reflects a simple mind. Actually a simple style is the result of hard work and hard thinking."

William Zinsser

Clarity is essential, but clarity alone does not make good workplace writing style. Also important are these three rules for workplace writing:

1. Be concise.
2. Use the right degree of formality.
3. Get straight to your point.

BE CONCISE

Have you ever been frustrated by someone who took ten minutes to say what he could have said in four or five? Don't frustrate your readers by taking too long to convey your message. Be *concise*. Concise means *brief, giving much information in few words*. On the sentence level, in general, *less* is more. The fewer words you use to get your point across, the better. Concise sentences are not only shorter than wordy sentences—they're also more clear. Below are three strategies for avoiding wordiness and writing concisely:

- eliminate clutter
- avoid unnecessary repetition
- use exact words and phrases

Eliminate Clutter

Avoid the following words, phrases, and constructions that add clutter to your writing.

1. **Because of the fact that.** In most cases, just "because" will do.

   Because of the fact that it rained, the game was canceled. (11 words)

   Because it rained, the game was canceled. (7 words)

2. ***That, which,* and *who* phrases** often clutter needlessly and can usually be rephrased more concisely. Try turning the *that, which,* or *who* phrase into an adjective.

   This is a manual *that is very helpful.* (8 words)

   This is a very *helpful* manual. (6 words)

   The meeting *which lasted five hours* ended at four. (9 words)

   The *five-hour* meeting ended at four. (7 words)

3. **There is, it is.** The *there is* and *it is* constructions avoid directly approaching the subject and use unnecessary words in the process. Instead, use a clear agent of action.

It is with regret that we must decline your kind offer. (11 words)

We regret that we must decline your kind offer. (9 words)

There is no reason we can find to disagree. (9 words)

We can find no reason to disagree. (7 words)

The revised versions are not only two words shorter—they're also more direct.

4.   That is a word that often clutters sentences unnecessarily. Sentences will often read more smoothly without it:

He said that he thought that the meeting was useful and that he was happy that there will be a follow-up meeting.
(23 words)

He said ~~that~~ he thought ~~that~~ the meeting was useful and that he was happy ~~that~~ there will be a follow-up meeting.
(20 words)

PRACTICE A
Revise the following sentences to eliminate clutter words, phrases, and constructions. Answers to all practice exercises are at the end of the chapter.

1.   The employees who were late missed the first set of awards.

2.   It is my feeling that we should hire her immediately.

3.   I believe that there is the possibility that the manager who was recently hired is not too fond of me.

Avoid Unnecessary Repetition

When writers are not sure that they've been clear, or when they are simply not being attentive to the need for concise writing, they often repeat themselves unnecessarily by saying the same thing in two different ways. This is what happened in the following example:

Wordy: We will meet at 4 p.m. in the afternoon. (9 words)

Concise: We will meet at 4 p.m. (6 words)

The abbreviation "p.m." *means* in the afternoon, so there's no reason to say "in the afternoon." It's a waste of words and of the reader's time.

Here are some more examples:

Wordy: The room is red in color. (6 words)

Concise: The room is red. (4 words)

Wordy: It is essential that everyone arrive promptly and on time. (10 words)

Concise: It is essential that everyone arrive on time. (8 words)

PRACTICE B

Eliminate unnecessary repetition in the following sentences.

1. It's time to terminate the project and put an end to it.
2. The car that is grey in color must have been in an accident or collision.
3. Please let me know your plans as soon as possible and at your earliest convenience.

Use Exact Words And Phrases

A lot of wordiness can often be trimmed by using *exact* words and phrases. This means substituting a strong, specific word for a weak, modified word or phrase. (A modifier is a word that describes, like *red* balloon or *very juicy* apple.) Notice how exactness cuts back on wordiness and makes for much more powerful sentences in the following examples:

He *walked very forcefully* into the room.

He **burst** into the room.

I *am not in agreement.*

I **disagree.**

Please *take a look at* our proposal.

Please **review** our proposal.

She was *very upset* by the news.

She was **devastated** by the news.

PRACTICE C

Revise the following sentences to make them more exact.

1. We are of the understanding that the deal is off.

2. He looked at the problem very carefully.

3. She is planning to say yes to the job offer.

USE THE PROPER LEVEL OF FORMALITY

Whenever you write, you must decide on the appropriate level of formality. Formality can range from very formal (proper, stuffy, distanced) to very informal (slangy, relaxed, intimate). In most cases, you should fall somewhere near the middle of the scale but slightly on the formal side. When you're writing email, however, you will often be on the informal end of the scale. Still, in most cases, you'll stay close to the middle.

In general, as the person you write to increases in rank, so should your level of formality. Also, the less familiar a person is to you, the greater your level of formality should be. Look at the following scale:

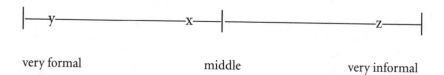

very formal   middle   very informal

When writing to your superior, even if you are friends, you should fall just to the left of the middle, around the "x". If, on the other hand, you write to the president of the United States, you might want to be somewhere near the "y" at the top of the scale. Similarly, in a letter to a close friend, your level of formality will probably be close to "z" at the other end of the scale.

How exactly does this translate for you as a writer? It mostly boils down to word choice. Look at the following sentences:

We would like to get a new computer.

We would like to buy a new computer.

We would like to purchase a new computer.

Get, buy, and *purchase* all mean essentially the same thing here, but they vary in degree of formality, with *get* being the least formal and *purchase* being the most formal. Thus, once you've established where you should fall on the formality scale, you need to choose your words accordingly.

PRACTICE D

Rank the following words in order of formality, with 1 being the least formal and 3 being the most formal:

___ permit
___ let
___ allow

__ remove
__ eliminate
__ get rid of

__ crash
__ collision
__ accident

GET RIGHT TO THE POINT

To say it once more: Time is money, so not only should you not waste your readers' time with wordiness, you should also not waste your reader's time with small talk. With the exception of email, when you write for work, *get right to the point.* If the person you are writing a memo to is also a close friend, talking about personal life may be okay, but in most cases, even friendly small talk in a memo is inappropriate. The memo below provides an example of inappropriate small talk.

TO:	Jennifer West
FROM:	Brenda East
DATE:	February 11, 2000
RE:	Purchase order for new computer monitor

How are you? I saw the picture that your son drew for you hanging in your office. It's wonderful! He'll be a great artist some day.

Anyway, I'm writing to ask about the purchase order I recently submitted for a new monitor...

First of all, you should probably *tell* Jennifer what you think of her son's drawing if you feel strongly enough to want to write about it. After all, a personal message is best delivered in person. Second, the first paragraph here has nothing to do with the matter at hand. If you wish to get personal or add a friendly comment or two, do it at the end of your letter or memo *after* you've taken care of business (in no case should there be a personal message in a report or proposal). You show more respect for your reader by getting straight to the point than by starting off with small talk. (Of course, email is the exception to this rule. See Chapter 17 if you need a review.)

Possible Answers to Practice Exercises
Practice A

1. The late employees missed the first set of awards.
2. I feel we should hire her immediately.
3. I believe the new manager may not be too fond of me.

Practice B

1. It's time to terminate this project.
2. The grey car must have been in an accident.
3. Please respond as soon as possible.

Practice C

1. We understand that the deal is void.
2. He studied the problem. Or: He scrutinized the problem.
3. She plans to accept the job offer.

Practice D

3. permit
1. let
2. allow

2. remove
3. eliminate
1. get rid of

1. crash
3. collision
2. accident

In Short

When writing for work, it's important to follow these rules of style:

- Be clear
- Be concise
- Use the right level of formality
- Get right to the point

Skill Building Until Next Time

Take one of the documents you wrote for a practice exercise in Section 3. Revise that document for clarity and for style.

CHAPTER | 22

Even the best writers don't get it right the first time. This chapter will teach you specific strategies for the all-important task of revising, or rewriting what you've written.

REVISING STRATEGIES

"The beautiful part of writing is that you don't have to get it right the first time, unlike, say, a brain surgeon."

Robert Cromier

Back in the introduction to this book, you read a statement that may have surprised you: writing *is* revising. The process of revision means just that: *re-vision*, to look at again. In other words, revising means reviewing what you've written to make sure that:

1. It does what it's supposed to do
2. It does it effectively

If it doesn't, or if it can be done better, you need to rewrite it.

Revising is a crucial step in the writing process. After prewriting and drafting your communication, you need to check its effectiveness on two different levels:

1. The big picture—ideas and organization.
2. The details—grammar, mechanics, and format.

This chapter deals with those big picture issues. Chapter 23 will help you edit the details of your documents effectively. The chapters are organized this way because this is the order in which revision should generally take place. If you go through a report correcting all of the sentence level problems before you check for a clear purpose and support, you might find that you have to rewrite much of the report anyway—so your time spent editing will have been wasted.

TWO HELPFUL HINTS FOR REVISING

Before you begin to look at specific "big picture" revising concerns, keep the following two guidelines for effective revising in mind.

Get Feedback

First, don't forget to *get feedback:* by reading aloud and showing your work to someone else. Reading your work aloud enables you to hear how your writing sounds and catch sections or sentences that are confusing, unclear, or grammatically incorrect. By showing your work to others, you can get objective feedback about how well you've fulfilled your purpose and how effectively you convey your information.

Give Yourself Time to Revise

Don't expect to write and revise a perfect memo or proposal in ten minutes. In fact, the earlier you begin your writing task, the better, because a little distance always helps. That is, if you draft your communication and then sit down to revise it right away, your draft may be too fresh in your head for you to think clearly about revisions. However, if you can put what you've written aside for a while—even if it's just for 15 minutes while you have a cup of coffee—when you come back, you will be able to think more clearly and creatively about what you've written and how to make it more effective.

REVISING STRATEGIES

Now to some specific revising strategies. Here is a list of things to look for when revising. It's important to address these issues in the order listed below so that you address the most global concerns (writing strategies that affect the whole document) before you focus in on more specific concerns (like the introduction and conclusion).

1. clear main idea
2. sufficient support
3. logical organization
4. readability factor
5. strong transitions
6. effective and appropriate introduction
7. effective and appropriate conclusion

Check for a Clear Main Idea

First, check for a clear main idea. Remember that your main idea should clearly convey the purpose of your communication, and this purpose should be made clear to your reader from the very beginning. You should look specifically for three things:

1. Is your main idea expressed in a clear topic sentence?
2. Is your main idea general enough to cover everything that you discuss in your communication?
3. Is your main idea expressed in one of the first sentences, if not the first?

If you answer "no" to any of these questions, go back and revise. For a review of how to clearly express your purpose in your main idea, see Chapter 3.

Check for Sufficient Support

Once you're sure you have a clear main idea, check that you've provided sufficient support for that idea. Remember that support can come from many sources, including:

details	comparisons
reasons	quotations or expert opinion
examples	statistics
results	descriptions
definitions	anecdotes

Whether your main idea is a matter of fact or a matter of opinion, you need supporting ideas to give your main idea credibility. Especially if you are trying to convince, the more support, the better.

You should also make sure that your support is the kind that you need to adequately fulfill your purpose. For example, if your purpose is to convince, have you shown your readers how they would benefit from agreeing to what you propose? Have you considered readers' reservations and objections? If your purpose is to complain, have you made it clear exactly what's wrong with the product, service, or item you're complaining about?

For a general review of how to provide strong support, see Chapter 4. For strategies for supporting different purposes, see the appropriate chapter in Section 2.

Check for Logical Organization

As you know by now, there are many organizing strategies writers can use to arrange their ideas logically. Here are the most common ones:

- chronological
- cause and effect
- spatial
- analysis/classification
- order of importance
- comparison and contrast
- problem and solution

If you read what you've written and the ideas seem out of order, or if it seems as if your communication jumps around, you should take a look at your organizing strategy. Is there one? Have you used it properly? Is it the most effective way to organize ideas in that document? For a review of organizing strategies, see Chapter 5.

Check for the Readability Factor

Remember the golden rule of workplace communications: *Always respect the reader.* This means, in part, making sure that your ideas are as easy for readers to follow as possible. One basic readability strategy is to organize information into small **chunks** of related ideas. Writers do this naturally by separating sentences into paragraphs. Related paragraphs should be chunked together in sections. Identify these chunks with short, clear **headings.**

Readability strategies also include using **lists, tables,** and **graphs.** As a general rule, if you have more than three items of information on one topic, you should use one or more of these readability strategies. Also, remember that how much you rely on these readability strategies depends upon the kind of document you're writing. An email, for example, should have smaller chunks and shorter paragraphs than a memo.

Check for Strong Transitions

Just as a train needs physical links between each railway car, when you write, your ideas need to be physically held together by transitions that show the relationship between your ideas. When you write without transitions, it's like asking your readers to jump from stone to stone across water because you haven't bothered to build them a bridge. So, check for strong transitions. Here are a few transitional words and phrases to jog your memory:

however	while
next	on the other hand
then	likewise
since	for example

A good way to check for strong transitions is to reread what you've written and circle all of the transitional words and phrases you can find. There should be several words that come from the list in Chapter 5 as well as others that are appropriate to the context of your message. If you seem to have very few words circled, you should probably check your writing again to see if connections between ideas could be stronger. For a review of transitions, see Chapter 5.

Check for an Effective and Appropriate Introduction

As much as you might wish otherwise, first impressions count, and how you introduce yourself to others can determine how others perceive (and receive) you. The same is true of writing. How you introduce your ideas can make a big difference in how your ideas are received.

When you're writing for work, the most common, practical, and sensible introduction is to begin with a clear topic sentence that states your purpose. That is, your opening sentences should:

- Tell readers the subject of your communication
- Tell readers the general idea that you want to convey *about* that subject

There are two ways you can accomplish this. The first and often the easiest method is to simply turn your purpose statement into a topic sentence. The second method is to rely, if possible, on a standard introductory phrase, like "I am writing in response to" or "As you requested."

If what you're writing is less serious or formal in nature and if it is something that you don't want to be overlooked, you can try a catchy introduction. Because so much of writing for work uses the types of introductions just mentioned, catchy introductions will really stand out. Catchy introductions, though, are most appropriate for informal workplace communications that aren't about important business matters. Be sure to use your judgment. For a review of introductions, see Chapter 19.

Check for an Effective and Appropriate Conclusion

Appropriately, the last item on the revising checklist is conclusions. How should you end a workplace communication? There are many specific strategies, but they all break down into two categories of conclusions:

- Conclusions that look back at what has been said or done
- Conclusions that look ahead to what will or should be done or what the writer expects to take place

Specifically, you could conclude by:

- summarizing or restating the main idea
- making recommendations
- stating what you're looking forward to
- asking or telling reader(s) to take a specific action
- providing a reference person for questions or future action
- thanking readers
- reminding readers why the matter is important to them

By looking ahead or looking back, you'll give readers a feeling of closure (that you've said all you have to say about the subject) and a feeling that your communication has amounted to something worthwhile for them. Thus, the stronger your concluding sentence(s), the better. For a more detailed review of conclusions, see Chapter 19.

PRACTICE

The following is a rough draft of a memo. Keeping in mind the purpose below, revise this memo using the strategies discussed in this chapter. You should be able to use all seven revising strategies.

Purpose: To point out a problem with theft of employee property and suggest ways to prevent future crimes.

Audience: Office Manager

There has been a lot of theft in our building recently. Yesterday I was a victim. It happened in the employee locker room. There are several ways we could reduce theft in the building. We could use combination locks instead of keys for lockers. Install cameras in key locations throughout the building. Hire more security officers. Hire an undercover employee. My watch and $10 were stolen from my jacket pocket. The locker room is the most common site of these thefts.

Possible Answer to Practice Exercise

This memo needs help in all seven areas:

1. It lacks a clear topic sentence that states the main idea of the memo.

2. It lacks sufficient support for its assertion that "there is too much crime in our building." We need to hear other examples of recent thefts. And the more detailed and specific those examples are, the better. How many thefts? Of what nature? When and where?

3. The information is not organized logically; the reader must jump from the problem to possible solutions and back to the problem again, and the problem itself—the specific incident—is not told in chronological order.

4. The possible solutions would be much more readable if they were in a list. The memo could also be divided into two separate sections—problem and solution.

5. There are few, if any, transitions between sentences in this paragraph.

6. This memo needs a clear, purpose-centered introduction. It could also begin with a catchy introduction, since it's an important but not formal subject and since it doesn't have to do with increasing the bottom line and therefore may get lost in the crowd.

7. It also needs a conclusion that looks ahead or looks back. It would be appropriate for this memo to look ahead and call for action.

Here is one way this memo could be revised:

I'm writing to call your attention to a very disturbing fact. In the last three months, there have been over a dozen incidents of theft on company property. Yesterday, I was the latest victim. My watch and $10 were stolen from my jacket pocket. I'd left my jacket in the employee locker room, which is the most common site of these thefts. In fact, there have been three thefts in the locker room in the last three weeks. Last week, Shannon Weil's purse was stolen, and two weeks before that, the present Roger White had bought for his wife during his lunch hour was stolen from the locker room. In addition, thefts have occurred in the lunchroom (employee lunches and thermoses) and in work areas. Arnold Proust, for example, had his calculator and $5 stolen from his desk drawer.

There are several simple measures we could take to reduce theft in the building. We could:

- Use combination locks instead of keys for lockers.
- Install cameras in key locations throughout the building.
- Hire more security officers.
- Hire an undercover detective to pose as an employee.

Clearly we have a security problem that must be addressed. Please consider implementing one or more of these security measures so that I will be the latest and the *last* victim.

IN SHORT

When you revise, begin with the "big picture" concerns: a clear purpose; strong, detailed support; logical organization; readability; strong transitions; and effective introductions and conclusions.

Skill Building Until Next Time

Are there things you've written recently that need revising? In what areas do they need the most work? If you notice a pattern (for example, several of your messages seem to lack sufficient support), you may want to review the corresponding chapter.

CHAPTER | 23

In addition to revising for content, writers need to edit their documents for correct grammar, mechanics, and format. This chapter will show you what to look for and how to correct your mistakes.

EDITING STRATEGIES

"The written word is often the first impression a business makes on a prospective customer or client. If it isn't spelled right, if it isn't punctuated right, if it doesn't look good on paper, the business loses credibility."

Lauren K. Anderson

Once you've revised for the "big picture," and revised your sentences for clarity and style, it's time to edit your document.

While revising deals with your ideas and how you express them, editing deals with grammar (correct sentences), mechanics (correct capitalization, spelling, and punctuation), and format (correct arrangement of text and graphics on the page). If you're satisfied that your document says what you want it to say, how you want to say it, then you're ready to make sure you present it clearly and correctly.

Below is a brief list of the editing issues reviewed in this chapter.

Revising vs. Editing

Revising focuses on the "big picture"—looking at your ideas, organization, and expression. Editing focuses on particular details, such as grammar, mechanics, and format.

Check for grammar:

- Are all sentences complete?
- Have you checked for run-on sentences?
- Are your verbs in the proper tense?

Check for mechanics:

- Are the proper items capitalized?
- Are sentences properly punctuated?
- Are all words spelled correctly? Have you checked for typing errors?

Check for format:

- Does your document have proper margins? Is it relatively centered on the page?
- Does your document have all of the parts it should have and in the order in which it should have them?
- Is your document printed neatly?

CHECK FOR GRAMMAR

Grammar refers to the rules that govern sentences. This is not a grammar book, and there isn't room here to review all of the rules you've learned over the years in school. But because clean, clear writing is so important, let's address three of the most common kinds of grammatical errors:

- Sentence fragments
- Run-on sentences
- Inconsistent tense

Sentence Fragments

A complete sentence has a **subject** (who or what performs the action) and a **verb** (a state of being or an action). It also expresses a complete thought. If you don't complete a thought, or if you are missing a subject or verb (or both), then you have a sentence fragment (an incomplete sentence). To correct a fragment, add the missing subject or verb or otherwise change the sentence to complete the thought.

Incomplete:	Which is true. [No subject. (*Which* is not a subject.)]
Complete:	*That* is true.

Incomplete:	For example, the waiting room and employee lounge. [No verb]
Complete:	Two examples *are* the waiting room and employee lounge.

Incomplete:	Even though we delivered the product on time. [Subject and verb, but not a complete thought.]
Complete:	We lost the contract even though we delivered the product on time.

Run-On Sentences

A **run-on** sentence occurs when two or more sentences run together without the proper punctuation between them. Usually, this means there's either no punctuation or just a comma separating the two thoughts. But commas alone are not strong enough to place between two complete ideas. Make sure you clearly separate your ideas by clearly separating individual sentences.

There are five ways to correct run-on sentences:

1. Use a period.
2. Use a comma and a conjunction: *and, or, nor, for, so, but, yet.*
3. Use a semi-colon.
4. Use a dash.
5. Use a dependent clause. Dependent clauses use words like *because, after, since, while,* etc.

Here's a run-on sentence corrected with each of the techniques listed above:

Run-on: Meet me at 2:00, I have to go over your report with you.
Corrections:
1. Meet me at 2:00. I have to go over your report with you.
2. Meet me at 2:00, **for** I have to go over your report with you.
3. Meet me at 2:00; I have to go over your report with you.
4. Meet me at 2:00—I have to go over your report with you.
5. Meet me at 2:00 **because** I have to go over your report with you.

Tense Shifts

A very common error, especially in reports or other communications that deal with events, is **shifting verb tenses**. That is, you start off describing an event in the present tense and then shift to the past tense (or vice versa). Make sure you're consistent; if you're talking about something that happened in the past, all of the verbs describing that event should be in the past tense.

Inconsistent:	Mr. Turner said he wouldn't leave until he talks to Mr. Francis.
Consistent:	Mr. Turner said he wouldn't leave until he talked to Mr. Francis.

Inconsistent:	When we get back to the front desk, he decides he didn't want to wait anymore.
Consistent:	When we got back to the front desk, he decided he didn't want to wait anymore.

CHECK FOR MECHANICS

Mechanics refers to the standard practices for the presentation of words and sentences, including **capitalization**, **punctuation**, and **spelling**. This isn't a book about mechanics, either, but let's review a few of the basics.

Capitalization

The general rule for capitalization is this: If you are referring to a **specific** person, place, or thing, the word should be capitalized. If you are referring to a **general** person, place, or thing, the word should not be capitalized.

Capitalized:	Our office is located on Elm Street in Williamstown.
Not capitalized:	Our office is located on a quiet street in a quiet town.

Capitalized:	I've registered for a course called New Strategies for Quality Control at Smithtown Technical College.
Not capitalized:	I've registered for a quality control class at a nearby college.

NOTE: Names of countries, languages, and nationalities should always be capitalized. Thus, if the sentence above read "My favorite subject has always been English," this sentence would be correct.

Punctuation

Punctuation marks are symbols used to separate ideas and make the meaning of sentences clear. Poor punctuation can lead to a great deal of confusion for your readers and can send a message other than what you intended. For example, take a look at the two versions of the following sentence:

Don't call me, stupid!
Don't call me stupid!

See what a difference punctuation can make? In the first sentence, the speaker is calling the listener "stupid." In the second sentence, the speaker is angry because the listener has called *him* "stupid."

There are many rules for punctuation, of course, and there isn't room to go into all of them here. However, the table below offers a few helpful guidelines for when to use which punctuation mark:

If Your Purpose Is To:	Use This Punctuation:	Example:
End a sentence	**period** [.]	Use a period to end a sentence.
Connect complete sentences	**semicolon** [;] or a **comma** [,] *and* a **conjunction** [and, or, nor, for, so, but, yet]	A semicolon can connect two sentences; it is an excellent way to show that two ideas are closely related.
Connect items in a list	**comma** [,] but if one or more items in that list already has a comma, use a **semicolon** [;]	The table was overturned, the mattress was torn apart, and the dresser drawers were strewn all over the floor.
		The castaways included a professor, who was the group's leader; an actress; and a housewife.

If Your Purpose Is To:	Use This Punctuation:	Example:
Introduce a quotation or explanation	**colon** [:] or **comma** [,]	Colons have three functions: introducing long lists, introducing quotations, and introducing explanations. He said, "This simply won't do."
Indicate a quotation	**quotation marks** [""]	"To be or not to be?" is one of the most famous lines from *Hamlet*.
Indicate a question	**question mark** [?]	Why are so many engineering students obsessed with *Star Trek*?
Connect two words that work together	**hyphen** [-]	brother-in-law, well-known author
Separate a word or phrase for emphasis	**dash** [—]	I never lie—never.
Separate a word or phrase that is relevant but not essential information	**parenthesis** [()]	There is an exception to every rule (including this one).
Show possession or contraction	**Apostrophe** [']	That's Jane's car.

Spelling

Presentation counts, and sometimes it counts for a lot. Always check your workplace documents for spelling and typographical errors. If you use a computer, run the spell check, or have someone else look over your document for spelling.

Even if you use spell check, make sure you read the text over, looking specifically for spelling errors and typos. Even the best spell check programs don't catch everything. For example, you may have typed "even" instead of "seven," but since "even" is a word, the spell checker won't catch that error for you.

Some writers find it easier to catch typos by "reading" backwards through their documents. Try this method if you think it might help.

CHECK FOR FORMAT

Because presentation counts, and counts for a lot, before you send your communication, check for proper formatting. Is your document properly laid out on the page?

General Formatting Guidelines

Each type of document has its own formatting specifications, but the formatting guidelines below apply to just about every document:

1. For documents of two or more pages, include page numbers.
2. Set 1 to 1½ inch margins on all sides. Don't run text too close to the edge of the page.
3. Use a 10- or 12-point standard font, such as Times New Roman or Arial. Never use a font that's difficult to read, like **Sand** or Peignot. They're fancy, but they're not reader friendly.
4. Avoid having one line of a paragraph standing alone at the top or bottom of a page.
5. Make sure you have a *clean*, clear printout to send—no faded toner.

In addition to following these general formatting guidelines, check to be sure your document follows the conventions for that type of document. For example, if it is a memo, does it have the proper heading? If it is a letter, does it have all of the necessary parts, in the proper order? See Section 3 for a review of particular workplace formats.

Practice

Revise and edit the following memo. You should be able to make corrections in most of the categories discussed in this chapter as well as those in Chapters 19–22.

MEMORANDUM

TO: John Jones, Quality Control Supervisor
FROM: Tim
DATE: 3/10/00
RE: Job

How are you? Fine, I hope.

Thank you for your kind letter of recommendation recommending me for the position of group leeder. Unfortunately, as you are probably already cognizant. the position was not received by me. It is my feeling that they wanted someone with more Experience. I am really down about it, but that doesn't mean I won't give it a shot next time.

Thank you again I appreciate your time and effort on my behalf.

Possible Answer to Practice Exercise
There are several problems with this memo:

1. The format of the TO/FROM lines don't match (one gives full name and title, the other just the first name).
2. The date is not written out properly.
3. The re: line is not specific enough.
4. The memo doesn't get straight to the point.
5. The sentence with "recommendation" and "recommending" has unnecessary repetition.
6. "Leeder" is spelled incorrectly.
7. "Cognizant" is pretentious language in this situation.
8. "Unfortunately, as you are probably already cognizant" is an incomplete sentence.
9. "The position was not received by me" is not an active sentence.
10. "It is my feeling that" is wordy because of the "it is" construction.
11. "They wanted" is a vague "they."
12. "Experience" should not be capitalized.
13. "Down about it" and "give it another shot" are too informal.

14. The last sentence is a run-on.

Here's one way you could correct these problems:

MEMORANDUM

TO:	John Jones, Quality Control Supervisor
FROM:	Tim Smith, Assembler
DATE:	March 10, 2000
RE:	Job Recommendation

Thank you for your kind letter recommending me for the position of group leader. Unfortunately, as you are probably already aware, I did not get the position. I believe that the production managers want someone with more experience. I am disappointed, but that doesn't mean I won't apply again next time.

Thank you again. I appreciate your time and effort on my behalf.

IN SHORT

If you want your writing to be well received, don't send it out without a careful edit. Check for correct grammar, mechanics, and format. Make sure your sentences are complete, ideas clear, and tenses correct. Check spelling, capitalization, and punctuation, and make sure your document is formatted properly. And don't forget that neatness counts.

Skill Building Until Next Time

Celebrate your completion of this book by thinking about everything you've learned. Compare something you wrote before you started this book to something you wrote in the last few days, and then congratulate yourself on your improvement.

APPENDIX A

WRITING SAMPLES FROM THE WORKPLACE

This appendix offers samples of real workplace writing from four organizations: The Department of Facilities Management at Polytechnic University, located in Brooklyn, NY; Creative Change of Hartford, CT; Gary Bilezikian Design of Brooklyn, NY; and Executive Car Service of Dallas, TX. The names and addresses of the writers and recipients of these communications have been changed.

The writing samples on the following pages include letters, memos, reports, and proposals as well as several emails and a complete Website.

SAMPLE MEMO

Brooklyn · Long Island · Westchester

MEMORANDUM

TO: Poly Community
FROM: Facilities Management
DATE: May 23, 2000
RE: Holiday Schedule

The following hours will be in effect for the Memorial Day Holiday:

SATURDAY, MAY 27, 2000
Rogers Hall & Dibner Bldg.   9 a.m. to 9 p.m.
Wunsch Bldg. / Student Ctr.   CLOSED

SUNDAY, MAY 28, 2000
Rogers Hall & Dibner Bldg.   9 a.m. to 9 p.m.
Wunsch Bldg. / Student Ctr.   CLOSED

MONDAY, MAY 29, 2000
Rogers Hall & Dibner Bldg.   9 a.m. to 9 p.m.
Wunsch Bldg. / Student Ctr.   CLOSED

PLEASE BE ADVISED—THE LIBRARY WILL BE CLOSED.

ALL FACULTY, STAFF, AND STUDENTS ARE REQUIRED TO HAVE
VALIDATED I.D. CARDS TO OBTAIN ENTRY TO THE BUILDINGS AND
MUST SIGN IN AND OUT AT THE SECURITY DESKS.

Please follow safety guidelines at all times and use the "buddy system."

Thank you.

SAMPLE MEMO

Brooklyn · Long Island · Westchester

MEMORANDUM

TO: Poly Community
FROM: Facilities Management
DATE: December 14, 1999
RE: Fire alarm testing on Sunday, December 19, 1999

On Sunday, December 19, 1999, Metro Fire Safety will be checking the fire alarms in all the buildings. They will be here from approximately 9 a.m. to 5 p.m.

If on Sunday you hear fire alarms, please disregard them unless you are otherwise instructed.

Thank you.

SAMPLE MEMO

Brooklyn · Long Island · Westchester

MEMORANDUM

TO: Security
FROM: Facilities Management
DATE: January 21, 2000
RE: Fire alarm testing on Sunday, January 23, 2000

On Sunday, January 23, 2000, Metro Fire Safety will be checking the fire alarm systems in all buildings. They will be here from approximately 9 a.m. to 5 p.m. Please notify Safety Alarm Company to take the system off line for the test and to put the system back on line when this is completed.

Thank you.

SAMPLE MEMO

Polytechnic
UNIVERSITY
Brooklyn · Long Island · Westchester

MEMORANDUM

TO: Kyle O'Donnell—Facilities Manager
FROM: Bill Drake
SUBJECT: Elevator Contract
DATE: July 22, 2000

As discussed, Up & Down Elevator Company has agreed to the following regarding their contract for maintenance with the University:

1) The yearly maintenance contract for five years, which was set to expire on March 31, 2001, will be canceled and a new one-year agreement will be put into effect as of August 1, 2000.

2) The new agreement will have a one-year renewal clause instead of five years. This change will not bind the University to a long-term commitment should circumstances change.

3) The annual maintenance charge will decrease from $16,7200.00 to $10,440,00, effective August 1, 2000.

I am awaiting the new contract agreement from Up & Down. However, the new payment schedule should go into effect as of August 1, 2000.

Let me know if you require any further information on this topic.

SAMPLE EMAIL

Subject: **Emergency Procedures**
Date: Thu, 27 Apr 2000 10:16:58 -0400 (EDT)
From: "Kevin O'Toole" <otoole@poly.edu>

The University has a Critical Incident Response Planning Committee that is reviewing all processes the University uses in planning for and responding to critical events. The following procedures describe the important steps an individual should take in the case of an emergency. These procedures are issued in anticipation of additional detailed plans to be disseminated by the Committee.

EMERGENCIES
In the event of an emergency situation, such as fire, smoke, gas smell, or injured person, an individual should immediately contact:
• the Facilities Management Office at extension 3020, or
• the Security Front Desk of Rogers Hall at extension 3537, or
• the Security Desk of the Dibner building at extension 3727.

Be prepared to give the room number and the building where the emergency is taking place. Please be specific. The Security Officer will be responsible for contacting the appropriate emergency agency. If nobody is available, contact the appropriate agency (primarily 911) and then contact the security supervisor or facility manager.

BOMB THREATS
The following are guidelines to assist an individual in handling a bomb threat received via telephone.
1. Remain calm on the telephone.
2. Try to obtain the following information from the caller:
   A. Location of the bomb
   B. Time the bomb is expected to go off
3. Note the current time on your watch.
4. Listen to the voice carefully and try to determine the following:
   A. The accent of the caller.
   B. The age of the caller.
   C. The sex of the caller.
5. Write down all your observations and the information given to you.
6. Try to recall the call type, whether internal or external, by noting the ring.
7. When the call is disconnected, immediately call the Office of Facilities Management at extension 3020.
8. Give as much information as possible to the person answering the phone in Facilities Management. That person will be responsible for contacting the authorities and initiating the evacuation procedure.
9. Continue to remain calm and follow standard evacuation procedure when the gong is activated.
10. Be available to answer any questions the authorities may have.

EVACUATION PROCEDURES

We would also like to take this opportunity to remind everyone of the emergency evacuation procedures for the University.

If you hear the fire bells ring, please exit the building immediately in an orderly fashion. Please use the stairwells and not the elevators to exit the building. Once outside the building, please stay a minimum of 100' from the building. In general it is best to go run an errand and come back later. It is very important to leave space for emergency vehicles.

Thank you for your cooperation.

University Facilities Management

SAMPLE EMAIL REPORT

Subject: Re: WALK THROUGH
Date: Fri, 14 Jan 2000 15:38:02 -0500
From: Glen Snyder <gsnyder@duke.poly.edu>
To: Amy Clark <aclark@duke.poly.edu>

Good afternoon.

This week the day custodians have been checking classrooms to be sure the correct amount of furniture is in each room. This is a very time consuming task as furniture is always moved around from room to room. They then need to search all rooms to re-organize the furniture.

All of the crafts personnel spent time in classrooms doing repairs, etc. pertaining to their craft. They have been able to work straight through without having to stop for a class.

The night custodians have been working on special cleaning of classrooms, etc. and will be finished this evening.

At the end of this month, we will be busy with many events. I have been working with the Registrar's office to try and head off conflicts I have come across.

I met with a company who does floor matting today. I would like to order entry mats with either our logo or university name. I will receive a proposal probably next week. I think this would really add a nice touch to all of our entrances. I'll have to see how much this would cost. I will let you know when I receive the proposal.

I also met with a cleaning supplies company. They feel they can set me up with a program for supplies, saving a substantial amount of money. I will meet with them again next week to go over some of the details.

That's it for now.

Until next week.

Glen

SAMPLE LETTER

Polytechnic
UNIVERSITY
Brooklyn · Long Island · Westchester

July 29, 2000

Mr. Leonard Klein
Bright Lights Electric Audits
133 Main Street
Bellevue, NY 11111

Dear Mr. Klein:

Thank you for all the documentation sent to me with your letter dated July 17, 2000 with reference to water and sewer credits and a refund application.

I have reviewed this entire matter and cannot understand why you are requesting a payment for credits the University has never received. Let me detail the facts in this situation from the documentation you sent as well as other information at my disposal.

The copies of the documentation you sent to me from the DEP indicate canceled charges for periods in 1989 through 1997. Apparently on September 7, 1988, you completed an application with the City of New York, Department of Finance for a "Request for Refund or Transfer of Credit" for a total of $22,586.13. This corresponds to the seven (7) copies of the DEP canceled charges from the documentation you submitted to me. From all the information given to me by your company as well as internal documents, it is obvious that a credit to our account or a check was never received. As a matter of fact, your March 21, 1999 letter to Mrs. Bell and your April 25, 2000 letter to me clearly reference the fact that you were pursuing a water and sewer refund and you assumed that a credit was transferred. However, you apparently do not have the means to substantiate that we received the amount in question.

With reference to the verification of the balance of a credit on our account, this amount is for $11,861.13, not the $22,586.13 you applied for in 1998. For your information, I have an analysis in 1999 from the NYC Water Board that clearly shows this credit belongs to items not specific to the 1989 through 1997 periods and ultimately that Bright Lights Electric Audits was not involved in assisting Polytechnic in these items.

Your letters constantly tell the University that you want to work with us in resolving past issues and to go forward in assisting us in our water and sewer audits. For the past few months, the difficulties in dealing with your organization in the matters reflected in this correspondence do not show Polytechnic that you can perform adequately in the areas you claim expertise.

Very truly yours,

Bill Drake
Director of Purchasing and
Business Management

SAMPLE LETTER

Creative **Change**

Creatively applying technology and design to assist clients
with changing and enhancing the way they do business.

May 12, 2000

Donald Thompson
WebWorld
341 Thompson Street
Hartford, CT 06011

Dear Donald,

Thank you for giving us the opportunity to review your client's new business
venture. Based on our experience and expertise in providing effective Internet
solutions, I believe we can help you build an effective prototype site for
YourAds.com.

Generally, we prefer to meet face-to-face with prospective clients in advance
of preparing a proposal for them. We've found that interaction and feedback
from such meetings gives us a much better sense of project parameters.
Given the urgency of presenting this information to your client, I realize this
wasn't possible. As you review this proposal, please know that I would be
happy to expand upon any of the concepts and ideas presented.

Feel free to contact me at 860-888-7777 or michael@cchange.com after you
have had a chance to review this proposal.

I look forward to hearing from you soon.

Sincerely,

Michael Paul
Vice President, Internet Business Development

SAMPLE PARTIAL PROPOSAL

Internet Design & Development Services

Prepared for Donald Thompson—YourAds.com

Proposal Contents

- Our Approach

- Internet Development Overview

- Services We Provide

- Project Scope, Customer Prototype Needs

- Technology Employed

- Proposed Services

- Terms and Conditions

SAMPLE PARTIAL PROPOSAL

Our Approach

At Creative Change, we seek to assist clients in communicating effectively with customers and employees via Internet and Intranet technologies. We accomplish this by getting to know you, your needs, and your customers' needs, and by understanding the technology required to help you reach your goals. Creative Change is able to offer an array of services that can provide full design, development and hosting for Internet and Intranet sites, or a component thereof which you may require through the key stages of Internet development. Through our partnership, we can help you harness the power of the Internet to accomplish your goals and objectives.

Internet Development Overview

Internet site development can be generally categorized into four key stages listed below. It's imperative to know your objectives for building a site, your audience, and the expected return for investing your time and money.

Informing

The first stage is a basic presence on the Internet to inform customers about who you are and what services you provide. The content is largely static in nature or may be updated quarterly and is often referred to as "Brochureware" in the industry. Although this is a necessary first step for your customers to get to know you better, it does not generate returns on the investment.

Marketing

This stage focuses on marketing with more interactive forms of technology. Examples include: interactive databases, dynamic event calendars, signup online, site-wide searching, etc. Customer data and site tracking should be captured to help you build a marketing database to further personalize data for your site in the next stage. This stage is also an investment to know your customers better and provide the stepping stone towards seeing profitable returns on your site.

Business Integration

This stage marks the beginning of seeing a return on your investment. Key technologies utilized help personalize information for customers, provide a high degree of interaction, and allow customers to transact services online. Examples include: customer profiles, e-commerce services, full order tracking, and beginning personalization services.

Business Transformation

This level creates a new way to do business via the Internet. It strives to integrate back-office functions, streamline customer interactions, and provide new ways of serving customers while reducing costs and the time needed to do so. While the cost to reach this level of operability is high, return on investment is typically substantial in this phase.

SAMPLE EMAIL

Date: Tue, 09 May 2000 14:43:20 -0400
From: "Michael Paul" <michael@cchange.com>
Reply-To: michael@cchange.com
Organization: Creative Change, Inc.
To: Beth Jenkins <beth_jenkins@client.org>
Subject: Captions for Photos?

Hi Beth-

Hope your meeting went well last week. I made several content changes to the site last week and am working with Jack Devlin, our artist, to add the new graphic pieces to the site this week. However, before he and I go too far with the photos, we were wondering if you could help us by creating some simple captions.

Please go to http://www.wellconnected.org/photos. There you will find the photos Jim and I selected for inclusion in your site. As soon as you have a chance, please review each one and see if you can come up with a brief caption that we could use. You can email me the captions, but please be sure to attach the photo number to each one.

OK, that's all for now. Talk to you soon!

--
Michael Paul
Vice President, Internet Business Development
Creative Change, Inc.
55 5th Street
Newton, CT 06001
Phone: 860.888.7777
Fax: 860.888.6666
Email: mailto:michael@cchange.com
Website: http://www.cchange.com

SAMPLE EMAIL

Subject: SHS Website
Date: Thu, 08 Jun 2000 17:16:50 -0400
From: "Michael Paul" <michael@cchange.com>
Organization: Creative Change, Inc.
To: Dave Brady <dave_brady@client.org>

Hi Dave-

It's been a little while since the last time you and I were in contact with each other. I think you helped me find a solution for Beth Jenkins in the Volunteer Services office, right?

In any event, Kyle Chesterfield spoke with my boss, Steven McBeal earlier today. Kyle suggested that we contact you regarding your Internet and/or Intranet projects. As you may know, we've been working on Internet initiatives with Corporate Communications and several other entities within your organization for a number of years now. If possible, we would like to catch up with you on Internet/Intranet plans for the future.

When you have a chance, please email or call me (860-888-7777 x11) to let me know when might be the best time for us to talk.

Thank you for your time, and I look forward to hearing from you.

--
Michael Paul
Vice President, Internet Business Development
Creative Change, Inc.
55 5th Street
Newton, CT 06001
Phone: 860.888.7777
Fax: 860.888.6666
Email: mailto:michael@cchange.com
Website: http://www.cchange.com

SAMPLE LETTER

George Brown Design
111 11th Street
Brooklyn, NY 11211

November 26, 1999

Paul Jackson
Work & Company, Inc.
123 Labor Drive
North Lake, PA 19991

Dear Paul,

On the following pages please find my bid for the Work & Company jobs as well as print bids from one of my printers. I broke the bid out into two sections, the Stationery and the Collateral Kit, as the Stationery is just straight production and should be considered separately. I'm still waiting on print bids from another printer, but these will give you a general idea of print costs. One note: the Open End Envelope bid, which is the large envelope, seems awfully high. I haven't spoken to my printer but it may be because we have four different lots. So just put that one aside until I speak to my printer about alternatives or have something to compare it to from another printer.

While reviewing your materials to come up with the bid, I realized that the only thing that is going to take any time to create is the brochure. Everything else is pretty straightforward. But based on our discussion of two versus one sample, I decided that it would not be worth it to only give you one. I feel that you need two design samples because you have your own ideas and concepts based upon previously created material, but I think it would be helpful if you had something to compare it to. Both will fit the look of your existing collateral and both will carry the same message. If you don't mind, I'd like to do one sample based on the separate folder and brochure, and another using the integrated folder/brochure concept. Additionally, I'd like to meet with you once more on the contents of the copy prior to starting the design. I think we need to streamline it some and focus on specific messages and information.

Call me with any questions/comments. I tried to keep the bid cost sensitive and believe that if we work out the contents of the brochure prior to starting the design, it should be a clean, straightforward job.

Yours truly,

George Brown

SAMPLE PROPOSAL

Proposal

CLIENT   Work & Company, Inc.
JOB   Collateral Kit, Stationery
CONTACT   Paul Jackson
DATE   September 26, 2000

OBJECTIVES

A. To create camera-ready artwork for Work & Company Inc. for their business cards and Canadian stationery. Design will match existing business cards and stationery with minor revisions to type and layout.

B. To create a collateral kit—envelope, one-color pocket folder, and two-color four-to-eight page brochure—for Work & Company Inc. whilch will match the existing look of the stationery system. Work & Company will supply George Brown Design (GBD) with text on disk for use in the brochure. GBD will, if necessary, work with Work & Company to streamline and focus the existing brochure copy. For the First Round Presentation, GBD will present two sample designs of the brochure and a mock-up of the folder. Second Round Presentation will be a revised version of the brochure chosen in round one. Folder mock-up will be similar to the existing report cover. GBD will negotiate print pricing and handle pre-press and print production (including press-check) to ensure successful completion of Work & Company's jobs.

PRICING

Business Cards and Stationery

DESCRIPTION	HOURS	HOURLY RATE	TOTAL
Layout and Production	5	$55	$275
Total			$275

Folder, Brochure and Envelope

DESCRIPTION	HOURS	HOURLY RATE	TOTAL
Design	16	$85	$1,360
Layout and Production	8	55	440
Administrative (print pricing/press-check)	8	45	360
Text Revisions (after second-round)	hourly	40	TBD
Total			$2,160

Schedule

First-round presentation	TBD
Second-round presentation	TBD
Final for proofing	TBD
Final to Printer	TBD

TERMS

- Estimates: all prices shown are estimates. Final fees and expenses shall be shown when invoice is rendered. Client's approval shall be obtained for any increases in fees or expenses. Estimate does not include costs for high-resolution color printouts for print proof, messenger and FedEx fees.
- 50% retainer to begin project. Remainder 30 days from delivery of final artwork to printer.
- Text revisions after second round: client changes billable at hourly rate.

SAMPLE LETTER

George Brown Design
111 11th Street
Brooklyn, NY 11211

July 13, 1999

Jeffrey Sanders
American Friends of Science
99 Research Lane
San Francisco, CA 94105

Dear Jeff:

Please find enclosed materials for the Spring-Summer issue of AFS's newsletter: a Zip disk with all the files, photos, artwork and fonts, and a color dummy of the Newsletter and Scientific Article pullout.

A few notes:

• This issue has an additional spread, as it's a double issue, so it will total 16 pages instead of 12.
• Nothing needs to be scanned at this time; all of the photos and artwork are on disk, placed in the QuarkXPress file, and ready to be output to film.
• The Scientific Article pullout is front and back of one page.
• Stan Jones is no longer with AFS, so unless otherwise noted, Margaret Anyawu will be your contact in terms of quantity, delivery date, blues, etc.

That's about it. I'm sending this to AFS prior to sending it to you. So if there are any corrections on either dummy, please input them prior to sending out film. Call if you have any questions. Hope all's well.

Best regards,

Helen Brown

SAMPLE LETTER

 George Brown Design
111 11th Street
Brooklyn, NY 11211

March 27, 2000

AdCopy Inc.
707 Elm Court
Lake Erie, PA 12345

Dear Sir/Madam:

Blair Schiller of Final Touch asked me to forward the enclosed mechanical which will be printed on a compact disk jacket. The reference number for this job is 149131.

If there are any problems with the artwork, I can be reached at (718) 222-3333. Otherwise, contact Blair Schiller for quantity, payment, and shipping instructions.

Sincerely,

George Brown

SAMPLE WEBSITE, PAGE 1

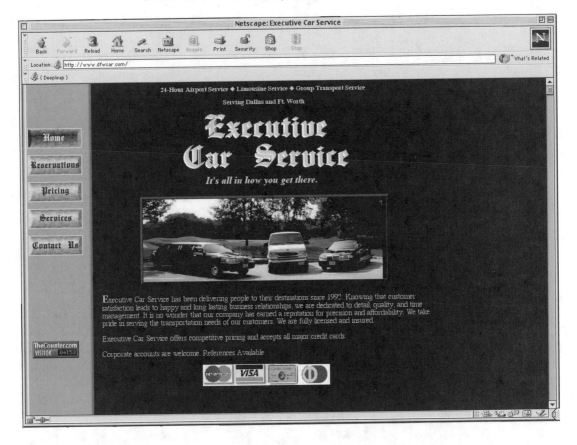

SAMPLE WEBSITE, PAGE 2

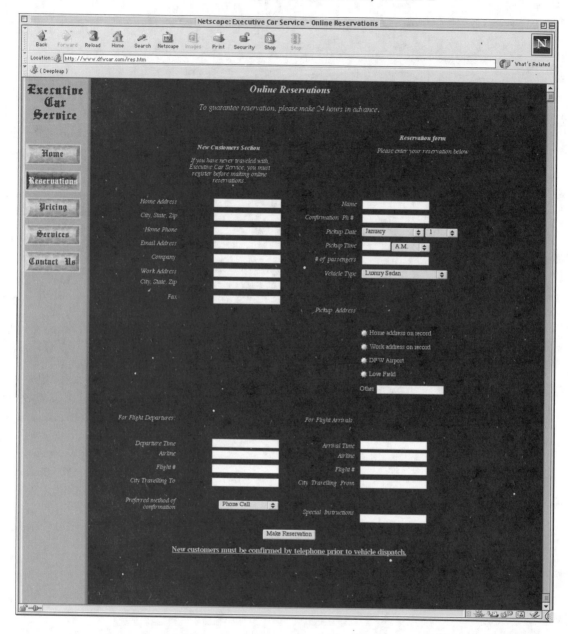

SAMPLE WEBSITE, PAGE 3

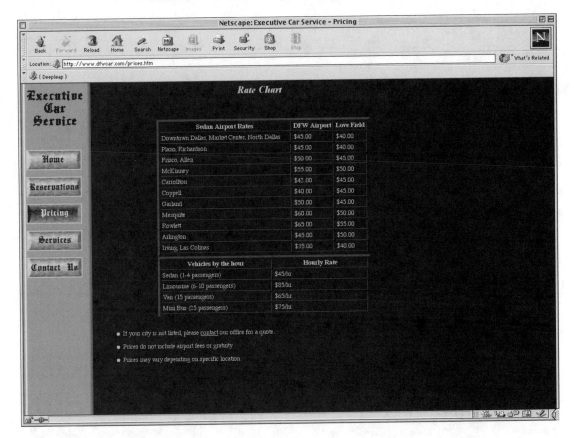

Netscape: Executive Car Service – Pricing

Location: http://www.dfwcar.com/prices.htm

Executive Car Service

- Home
- Reservations
- Pricing
- Services
- Contact Us

Rate Chart

Sedan Airport Rates	DFW Airport	Love Field
Downtown Dallas, Market Center, North Dallas	$45.00	$40.00
Plano, Richardson	$45.00	$40.00
Frisco, Allen	$50.00	$45.00
McKinney	$55.00	$50.00
Carrollton	$42.00	$45.00
Coppell	$40.00	$45.00
Garland	$50.00	$45.00
Mesquite	$60.00	$50.00
Rowlett	$65.00	$55.00
Arlington	$45.00	$50.00
Irving, Las Colinas	$35.00	$40.00

Vehicles by the hour	Hourly Rate
Sedan (1-4 passengers)	$45/hr
Limousine (6-10 passengers)	$85/hr
Van (15 passengers)	$65/hr
Mini Bus (25 passengers)	$75/hr

- If your city is not listed, please contact our office for a quote.
- Prices do not include airport fees or gratuity.
- Prices may vary depending on specific location.

SAMPLE WEBSITE, PAGE 4

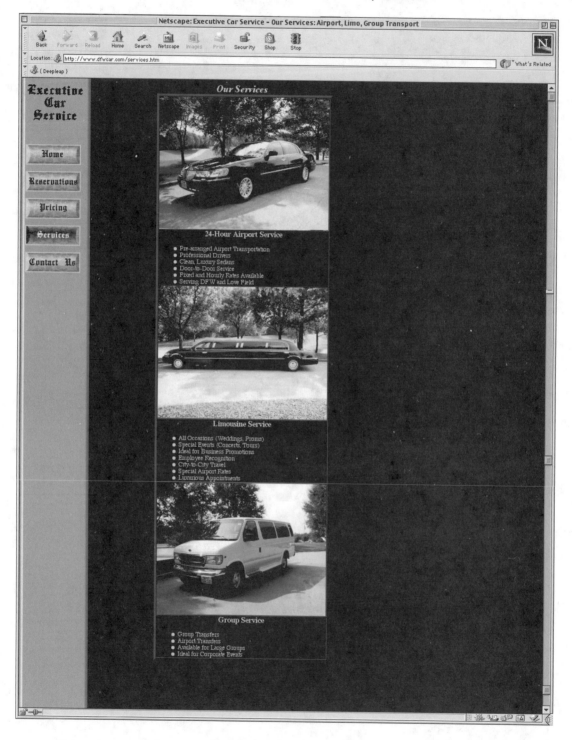

SAMPLE WEBSITE, PAGE 5

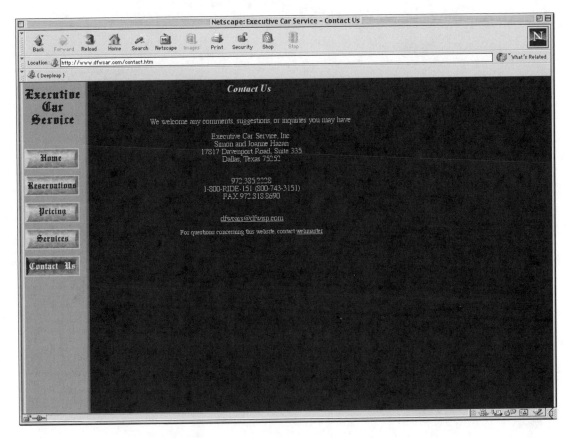

APPENDIX | B

ADDITIONAL RESOURCES

There are lots of other books that can help you with your writing. Most of the books listed in this appendix focus specifically on business writing, but some are geared to almost any kind of writing. If you feel you still need to sharpen your skills after reading this book, try one or more of the books listed below.

Allen, Jo. *Writing in the Workplace.* Allyn & Bacon, 1997.

Alread, Gerald, Brusaw, Charles, and Walter E. Oliu. *Writing that Works: How to Write Effectively on the Job.* 5th ed. New York: St. Martin's Press, 1995.

Angell, David, and Brent Heslop. *The Elements of E-Mail Style: Communicate Effectively Via Electronic Mail.* Addison-Wesley, 1994.

Bailey, Jr., Edward P. *Plain English at Work: A Guide to Writing and Speaking.* New York: Oxford University Press, 1996.

Bates, Jefferson D. *Writing with Precision: How to Write So That You Cannot Possibly Be Misunderstood.* Penguin, 2000.

Baugh, L. Sue, Maridell Fryar, and David A. Thomas. *How to Write First-Class Business Correspondence: The Handbook for Business Writers.* Lincolnwood, IL: NTC, 1995.

Baugh, L. Sue. *How to Write First-Class Memos: The Handbook for Practical Memo Writing.* Lincolnwood, IL: NTC, 1995.

Bell, Arthur H. *Complete Business Writer's Manual: Model Letters, Memos, Reports and Presentations for Every Occasion.* 2nd ed. Englewood Cliffs, NJ: Prentice Hall, 1996.

Bernhardt, Stephen, and Edward L. Smith. *Writing at Work: Professional Writing Skills for People on the Job.* Lincolnwood, IL: NTC, 1997.

Blake, Gary. *Quick Tips for Better Business Writing.* New York: McGraw Hill, 1995.

Blicq, Ron. *Communicating at Work: Creating Messages that Get Results.* Englewood Cliffs, NJ: Prentice Hall, 1991.

Brereton, John, and Margaret A. Mansfield. *Writing on the Job: A Norton Pocket Guide.* Norton, 1999.

Cormier, Robin. *Error-Free Writing : A Lifetime Guide to Flawless Business Writing.* Prentice Hall, 1995.

Ferrara, Cosmo F. *Writing on the Job: Quick, Practical Solutions to All Your Business Writing Problems.* Englewood Cliffs, NJ: Prentice Hall, 1995.

Flower, Linda, and John Ackerman. *Writers at Work: Strategies for Communications in Business and Professional Settings.* Harcourt, Brace, Jovanovich, 1997.

Griffin, Jack. *The Complete Handbook of Model Business Letters.* Prentice Hall, 1997.

Guffey, Mary Ellen. *Business Communication: Process and Product.* 3rd ed. South-Western Publishing, 1999.

Hamper, Robert, and L. Sue Baugh. *Handbook for Writing Proposals.* NTC Publishing Group, 1996.

Harty, Kevin. *Strategies for Business and Technical Writing.* 4th ed. Allyn & Bacon, 1998.

Heller, Bernard. *The 100 Most Difficult Business Letters You'll Ever Have to Write, Fax, or E-Mail.* Harperbusiness, 1994.

Kilian, Crawford. *Writing for the Web.* Self-Counsel Press, 2000.

Kolin, Philip C. *Successful Writing at Work.* 4th ed. Lexington, MA: D.C. Heath & Co., 1993.

Lauchman, Richard. *Plain Style: Techniques for Simple, Concise, Emphatic Business Writing.* New York: Amacom, 1993.

Layton, Marcia. *The Complete Idiot's Guide to Terrific Business Writing.* New York: Macmillan, 1996.

Lindsell-Roberts, Sheryl. *Business Writing For Dummies®.* IDG Books Worldwide, 1999.

Lundsford, Andrea, Robert Conners, and Franklin Horowitz. *Easy Writer: A Pocket Guide.* Bedford Books, 1997.

Lutovich, Diane, and Janis Fisher Chan. *How to Write Reports and Proposals.* Advanced Communication Designs, 1998.

McCormick, Donald, and Phyllis Hemphill. *Business Communication with Writing Improvement Exercises.* 5th Ed. Prentice Hall, 1996.

Muckian, Michael, and John Woods. *Business Letter Handbook: How to Write Effective Letters & Memos for Every Business Situation.* Adams Media Corporation, 1993.

Pearsall, Thomas. *How to Write for the World of Work.* 6th ed. New York: Harcourt Brace, 2000.

Pincu, Gloria. *Bull's Eye Business Writing: 10 Easy Guides for Getting to Your Writing Target.* 2nd ed. BLS Publishing, 1999.

Pitrowski, MaryAnn V. *Effective Business Writing: A Guide for Those Who Write on the Job.* New York: Harper Collins, 1996.

Poe, Roy W. *The McGraw-Hill Handbook of Business Letters.* 3rd ed. New York: McGraw Hill, 1994.

Prentice Hall's Get a Grip on Writing: Critical Skills for Success in Today's Business Writing. Englewood Cliffs, NJ: Prentice Hall, 1996.

Raimes, Ann. *Keys for Writers: A Brief Handbook.* Boston: Houghton Mifflin, 2000.

Reid, James, and Anne Silleck. *Better Business Letters: A Self-Instructional Book to Develop Skill in Writing.* Addison-Wesley, 1990.

Rice, Judith R. *Learning Workplace Writing.* Englewood Cliffs, NJ: Prentice Hall, 1994.

Roth, Audrey J. *The Elements of Basic Writing.* Boston: Allyn and Bacon, 1994.

Saben, Tim J. *Practical Business Communication.* Homewood, IL: Irwin Professional Publications, 1994.

Saltzman, Joel. *If You Can Talk, You Can Write: A Proven Program to Get You Writing and Keep You Writing.* New York: Warner Books, 1993.

Strunk, William, and E. B. White. *The Elements of Style.* 3rd ed. New York: Macmillan, 1979.

Stuckey, Marty. *Basics of Business Writing.* New York: Amacom Book Division, 1992.

Theibert, Philip. *Business Writing for Busy People.* Career Press, 1996.

Venolia, Jan. *Rewrite Right! : How to Revise Your Way to Better Writing.* Ten Speed Press, 1987.

Vitanza, Victor. *Writing for the World Wide Web.* Allyn & Bacon, 1997.

Wienbroer, Diana Roberts, et al. *Rules of Thumb for Business Writers.* McGraw-Hill, 1999.

Williams, Joseph M. *Style: Ten Lessons in Clarity and Grace.* 6th Ed. New York: Longman, 1999.

Wilkie, Helen. *Message Received and Understood!* MHW Communications, 1999.

Zinsser, William. *On Writing Well: The Classic Guide to Writing Nonfiction.* Harper Collins, 1998.

INDEX

A

abusive language, 87
active voice, 209–211
addresses, in letters, 125–126
adjusting and correcting,
89–90
analysis/classification, 37–38
anticipating objections, 116
assertions, support for,
108–109

B

block technique, 40–41
body
of instructions, 101
of letter, 127
of memo, 140–147
of reports, 151

C

capitalization, 236–237
in e-mail, 174
cc/distribution line, 129–130,
140
chunking information, 51–52
clarity, 75–84, 99–100,
203–211, 213
active voice in, 209–211
ambiguous language,
avoiding, 207–208
jargon, avoiding, 204–206
pretentious language,
avoiding, 206–207
and proper tone of voice,
77
unclear pronoun
references, avoiding,
208–209

classification, organization by,
37–38
close, of letter, 127–128
comparison and contrast,
40–41
complaining, 86–89
complaints, sample memos of,
88–89
conclusions, 101, 141,
151–152, 199–202
revision of, 228
thank-you messages, 200
conclusions.
See also introductions.
congratulating, 81–83
content, 5
convincing, 113–119
anticipating objections
and, 116

convincing *(continued)*
    and catchy introduction,
        117–118
    prewriting and, 114
    providing evidence,
        115–116
    and requesting action,
        116–117
    showing benefits of, 115
correcting and adjusting,
    89–90

D

date line, 126, 139–140
demanding, 91–95
distribution line, 129–130,
    140

E

editing, 233–241
    capitalization, 236–237
    formatting, 239–241
    mechanics of grammar,
        234–239
    punctuation, 237–238
    revising vs., 234
    run-on sentences, 235
    sentence fragments, 234
    spelling, 238
    verb tenses, 236
electronic mail(e-mail), 167
    appropriate use of, 169
    capitalization in, 174
    effective writing of,
        170–177
    emoticons, 174
    formality in, 172–173
    formats of, 168, 175
    graphs in, 176
    headings, 175
    length considerations, 171
    lists in, 175
    nature of, 168
    proper tone of, 173
    report sample, 250
    samples of, 248–250,
        257–258

    tables in, 176
    typographical clues, 174
emoticons, 174
enclosure, with letter, 129
errors, responding to, 89–90

F

facts, 19, 22
    support for, 26–28,
        108–109, 151–152,
        225–226
feedback, 3–4, 224
file number, 128
following up, 80–81
formality, 144–146
format, 11, 234
    editing, 239–241
    for e-mail, 168, 175
    for memos, 146
    for reports, 150
"from" line, in memos, 139

G

grammar and mechanics, 5,
    234–239
graphs, 56–61
    in e-mail, 176
    in websites, 187

H

headings, 53–55
    in e-mail, 175
    guidelines for, 54–55
    in memos, 138
    in reports, 151
    in websites, 187
home pages, 180, 185–186
hypertext, 180

I

"I" vs. "you," in complaints,
    87–88
importance, organization by,
    38–40
incident reports, 154–155
information, chunking
    information, 51–52
informing, 78–79

inquiring, 79–80
introductions, 195–202
    catchy, 117–118
    introductory phrases,
        197–199
    and memos, 141–146
    parts of instructions,
        100–101
    in reports, 151
    revision of, 228
    topic sentences, 196
introductions. *See also*
    conclusions.

J

jargon, 204–206

L

letters, 123–135
    formats of, 130–134
    neatness in, 124–126
    parts of, 125–130
    samples of, 251–253, 259,
        261–262
    of two or more pages, 133
links, 180
lists, 55–56, 99
    in e-mail, 175
    in websites, 187

M

main idea, 17–24
    support structures for,
        19–21, 25–32, 108–109,
        151–152, 225–226
meeting minutes, 155–157
memos, 137–148
    body of, 140–147
    formality of, 144–146
    headings of, 138–139
    samples of, 244–247

N

navigation bars, 184
neatness, 124–126
negative messages, conveying,
    85–95

O

objectivity, in reporting, 71–72
observation, in reporting, 70–71
opinion, 19–22, 28, 108–109
    support for, 28–31, 226
organization, 5, 33–47
    analysis/classification, 37–38
    cause and effect, 35–36
    chronological/sequential, 34–35
    comparison and contrast, 40–41
    and memos, 141–146
    order of importance, 38–40
    problem/solution, 42
    revision of, 226–227
    spatial relations and, 36–37

P

point-by-point technique, 40–41
positive or neutral message, conveying of, 75–85
prewriting, 12–13, 114
problems
    and problem/solution organization, 42
    in proposals, 161
procedures and instructions
    clarity and, 99–100
    completeness in, 102–103
    parts of, 100–101
    readers of, 97–98
    samples of, 101–102
    testing and, 103–105
    thoroughness in, 98–99
progress reports, 152–153, 158
proofreading, websites, 187
proposals, 159–165
    goals of, 163
    problem statement, 161
    readers of, 160–161
    sample of, 162–163, 254–256, 260

solution budget, 162
solution descriptions, 161
solution time lines, 162
types of, 160
punctuation, 237–238
purpose, 11, 21–22
    clarification and, 76
    of proposal, 163
    of report, 150
    statement of (topic of sentence), 22–24

R

readability strategies, 49–63
    headings, 53–55
    practice exercises, 61–63
readers (audience), 10
    conveying negative messages to, 85–95
    feedback from, 3–4
    instructions for, 97–98
    respect for, 86–89
recommendations, in reports, 151–152
rejecting and refusing, 90–91
reminding, 77–79, 91–95
reports, 67–74, 149–158
    accuracy, 68
    e-mail, sample of, 250
    formats for, 150
    incident reports, 154–155
    of meeting minutes, 155–157
    practice exercises, 72–74
    progress reports, 152–153
    thoroughness, 68–69
requesting, 79–80
responding, 80–81
reviews, 107–111
    good and bad qualities addressed in, 109–111
    support for assertions in, 108–109
revising, 4, 223–231
    clarity of main idea, 225–226
    conclusions, 228–229
    editing vs., 234
    feedback, 224

and getting feedback, 4
grammar and mechanics, 5
introductions, 228–229
making time for, 224
organization, 226
for readability, 227
support for main idea, 226
websites, 187
words and phrases, 227–228
run-on sentences, 235

S

salutation, 127
sentence fragments, 234
signature, of letter, 128
site maps, 181
solution descriptions, in proposals, 161
spelling, 238
steno line, 128
style, 5, 11, 213–221
    concise writing and, 213–217
    exact words and phrases, use of, 216–217
    formality and, 217–219
    and getting to the point, 219–220
    repetition, avoiding, 216
subject, 10, 18–19, 216
subject line (re: line), in memos, 139–140

T

tables, 56–61
    in e-mail, 176
    in websites, 187
thanking, 81–83
thoroughness, 98–99
"to" line, in memos, 138–139
tone of voice, 77
transitional words and phrases, 43–44
transitions, 42–46
trip reports, 155
typographical clues, in e-mail, 174

V

verb tenses, shifted, 236

W

warnings, 99–100
websites, 179–191
   formality in, 187
   graphs in, 187
   headings, 187
   home pages, 180, 185–186
   hypertext, 180
   information organization
      on, 181–186
   links, 180
   lists in, 187
   navigation bars, 184
   revisions to, 187
   sample of, 263–267
   scanning, 187
   site maps, 181
   tables in, 187
   text writing guidelines,
      187–188
welcoming, 81–83
workplace writing, 9–16,
   167–168
   additional resources for,
      269–273
   comparison and contrast,
      40–41
   conveying a positive or
      neutral message, 75–84
   elements of, 9–11
   graphs and tables, 56–61
   practice scenarios, 13–16
   readability strategies,
      49–63
   support structures for,
      19–21
   transitions, 42–46

Y

"you" vs. "I," in complaints,
   87–88

Master the Basics... Fast!

Easy to Use & Understand

If you need to improve your basic skills to move ahead either at work or in the classroom, then our LearningExpress books are designed to help anyone master the skills essential for success. It features 20 easy lessons to help build confidence and skill fast. This series includes real world examples—**WHAT YOU REALLY NEED TO SUCCEED.**

All of these books:

• Give quick and easy instruction

• Provides compelling, interactive exercises

• Share practical tips and valuable advise that can be put to use immediately

• Includes extensive lists of resources for continued learning

---

Write Better Essays
208 pages • 8 1/2 x 11 • paper
$13.95 • ISBN 1-57685-309-8

Read Better, Read More, 2e
208 pages • 7 x 10 • paper
$14.95 • ISBN 1-57685-336-5

Grammar Essentials, 2e
208 pages • 7 x 10 • paper
$14.95 • ISBN 1-57685-306-3

The Secrets of Taking Any Test, 2e
208 pages • 7 x 10 • paper
$14.95 • ISBN 1-57685-307-1

Math Essentials, 2e
208 pages • 7 x 10 • paper
$14.95 • ISBN 1-57685-305-5

Improve Your Writing For Work, 2e
208 pages • 7 x 10 • paper
$14.95 • ISBN 1-57685-337-3

How To Study, 2e
208 pages • 7 x 10 • paper
$14.95 • ISBN 1-57685-308-X

To Order: Call 1-888-551-5627

Also available at your local bookstore. Prices subject to change without notice.

LearningExpress • 900 Broadway, Suite 604 • New York, New York 10003

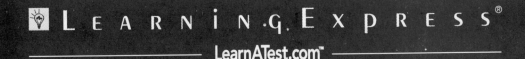
LEARNING EXPRESS®
LearnATest.com™